PICKER'S
POCKET·GUIDE

U.S. COINS
& CURRENCY

How to Pick Antiques like a Pro

ARLYN G. SIEBER

Published by

Krause Publications, a division of F+W Media, Inc.
700 East State Street • Iola, WI 54990-0001
715-445-2214 • 888-457-2873
www.krausebooks.com

To order books or other products call toll-free 1-800-258-0929
or visit us online at www.krausebooks.com

ISBN-13: 978-1-4402-4657-9
ISBN-10: 1-4402-4657-2

Cover Design by: Rebecca Vogel
Designed by: Dane Royer
Edited by: Paul Kennedy

Printed in China

10 9 8 7 6 5 4 3 2 1

Picker's Tip

What makes a coin valuable? Rarity and condition working in concert can bring eye-popping prices. A rare or scarce coin can be valuable in just about any grade. But a relatively common coin can be valuable if it's rare in the top uncirculated grades. A 1946-S quarter in grade MS-65 sells for about $35, but in early 2011, an example of the same issue graded MS-68 by the Professional Coin Grading Service (PCGS) brought a stunning $14,950 at auction.

1913 Liberty Nickel

Coins Introduction

An armed guard stood outside the door to the coin show's security room as six of the nation's top numismatic experts prepared to make hobby history. For decades, only four examples of the 1913 Liberty nickel were known to exist, but now the experts were examining a possible fifth example. Rumors of a fifth specimen extant focused on a North Carolina coin dealer who died in a car accident in 1962. His heirs were told after his death that the coin was a fake, but they kept it and brought it forth to be re-examined in 2003.

The six experts carefully compared the coin's diagnostics with the four known specimens and with known fakes. Their unanimous conclusion was that the coin was indeed genuine. Several years later, it sold at auction for more than $3.1 million.

In February 2013, a couple were walking their dog on their northern California property when they noticed an old can sticking up out of the ground. They dislodged it with a stick and brought it back to their house. They pried open the lid and were shocked to discover it was filled with 19th-century gold coins. They went back to the site and subsequently discovered seven more cans filled with gold coins. More than 1,400 coins were discovered in all, and the hoard was valued at about $10 million. Among the coins was a rare 1866-S gold $20 without the motto "In God We Trust" on the reverse, valued at $1 million.

Extreme examples? Certainly. But they illustrate the rewards that await those who know what to look for when they happen upon a stash of old coins or paper

The Saddle Ridge Hoard

David Hall, co-founder of Professional Coin Grading Service, poses with some of 1,427 Gold-Rush era U.S. gold coins, at his office in Santa Ana, Calif., Tuesday, Feb. 25, 2014. *Associated Press Photo*

The Saddle Ridge Hoard will go down in history as one of the most stunning, intriguing and generally mind-blowing picks of all time. After all, how many people stumble across 1,400 Gold-Rush era coins worth more than $10 million in their yard?

The answer: two, and they live in Northern California. The middle-aged couple, who requested anonymity, unearthed eight cans filled with gold coins buried in the shadow of an old tree on their property in 2013. The treasure trove of coins dating from 1847 to 1894 included four $5 gold pieces, 50 $10 gold pieces, and 1,373 $20 double eagles. The prize of the find: an 1866-S No Motto $20 gold piece valued at more than $1 million.

The face value of the discovery was $27,980 – a goodly sum but light years from its collector value. Professional Coin Grading Service (PCGS), who authenticated the coins, reported that many were recovered in uncirculated, mint condition. The coins were seemingly stashed immediately after they were minted, making the hoard worth millions to collectors today.

Most of the coins were minted at the San Francisco Mint. Who put them there is a mystery that may never be solved. Some claimed the coins were buried by outlaw Jesse James, or perhaps stagecoach robber Black Bart, or even stolen from the San Francisco Mint. But those theories, and others, have been dismissed.

"We all dream about discovering buried treasure; seeing the real thing in person – piles of gold coins encrusted in dirt and rust – the experience was just indescribable," said David McCarthy, a numismatist with Kagin's, the California firm which handled the initial evaluation of the coins and assessed the significance of the find. "Never in my wildest dreams would I imagine coins coming out of the ground in the kind of condition that I saw in front of me. Many pieces were finer than anything known in major collections or museums."

The stash found on land the couple nicknamed Saddle Ridge is the largest such discovery in U.S. history. One of the largest previous finds of gold coins was uncovered by construction workers in Jackson, Tenn., in 1985 and valued at $1 million. More than 400,000 silver dollars were found in the home of a Reno, Nevada, man who died in 1974 and were later sold intact for $7.3 million.

money. And they don't even have to be old to be valuable. Scarce varieties of modern coins are discovered
too. Take, for example, the 2004 Wisconsin quarter in the
U.S. Mint's 50 States Quarters series.

In early 2005, a number of the quarters with a "D"
mintmark for the Denver Mint were discovered with
what appears to be an extra leaf in the ear of corn on
the reverse. The extra leaf appears to the viewer's left of
the ear of corn beneath the large turned-down leaf. As
the coins surfaced, two varieties were detected: One has
the extra leaf pointed downward (listed as "leaf low" in
some value guides), and the second has the extra leaf
pointed upward ("leaf high").

How did it happen? According to the U.S. Mint's
official report on the incident, a press operator at the
Denver Mint noticed blemishes on the Wisconsin quarters being produced on one of the five machines he was
operating. He stopped the machine but then left for a

EXTRA LEAF LOW   **EXTRA LEAF HIGH**

meal break before correcting the problem.

When he returned to work, the machine was running
again, so he assumed that another worker had changed
the working die being used to strike the quarters. About
an hour and a half later, it was discovered the problem
had not been resolved and that thousands of coins
with the extra leaf had been struck and comingled with
regular coins produced by other presses. By the time the

mistake was discovered, the coins were already bagged and ready for shipment.

In circulated grades, the coins' retail value ranges from $50 to $100. The "leaf high" variety is more scarce than the "leaf low" variety and commands slightly higher values.

What other numismatic treasures are out there waiting to be picked? Here's a quick guide of some things to watch for:

SILVER COINS. Until 1965, U.S. dimes, quarters, and half dollars were struck in the traditional composition of 90-percent silver and 10-percent copper. In late 2015, silver was trading at about $15 a troy ounce. That made the silver in a pre-1965 quarter worth about $2.70. Although most of the old silver coinage has been culled from circulation over the years, silver coins of current design (Roosevelt dimes, Washington quarters, and Kennedy half dollars) still slip through now and then.

1965-1970 KENNEDY HALF DOLLARS. Although silver was eliminated from dimes and quarters starting with 1965-dated coins, Kennedy half dollars continued to contain a reduced amount of silver through the 1970-dated coins. The composition of Kennedy half dollars dated 1965 through 1970 is 40-percent silver, or 0.148 troy ounces.

KEY DATES. Scan the value listings for a series of coins and you'll see some dates and mintmarks that stand out from the rest. These issues are more scarce and, as a result, command higher values. They're known as "key dates" in hobby lingo. Some examples include the 1931-S Lincoln cent, the 1950-D Jefferson nickel, and the 1932-D Washington quarter. Knowing these key dates when searching a hoard of old coins can help a picker select the more valuable from the ordinary.

ERROR COINS. Sometimes the U.S. Mint makes mistakes when producing coins. Modern minting methods have reduced the errors, but as demonstrated by the 2004 Wisconsin quarter, they can still occur. Errors and minting varieties are still discovered on older coins too.

Take, for example, the 1982 no-mintmark dime. All dimes produced for circulation in that year are supposed to have a mintmark, either a "P" for the Philadelphia Mint or a "D" for Denver Mint. A working die without a "P" mintmark was mistakenly put into production at Philadelphia and apparently went unnoticed for a significant period.

Today the 1982 no-mintmark dime is worth about $30 to $60 in typical circulated grades. Note that this

error applies only to the 1982-dated dime. Dimes struck at Philadelphia prior to 1980 do not have mintmarks and are not supposed to have mintmarks.

Many other error coins exist. For detailed descriptions and photos, see the book *Strike It Rich With Pocket Change* by Brian Allen and Ken Potter (Krause Publications).

PAPER MONEY. Paper money isn't as durable as coins and does not contain precious metal, so chances of finding a survivor with any significant value are lessened. But old bills still pop up now and then in a previously hidden stash. As with key dates in coins, scan the paper-money listings in this guide for key issues – those with values that stand out from the rest. Occasionally, small-size silver certificates still show up in circulation. They look similar to today's Federal Reserve notes but say "Silver Certificate" at the top of their faces instead of "Federal Reserve Note." Silver certificates are no longer redeemable for silver, but some are valued significantly above their face values.

HANDLE WITH CARE

If you do find a collectible coin or piece of paper money, handle it with care. Coins should be handled by their edges between your thumb and forefinger. Do not fold paper money; leave it flat.

Put the coin or piece of paper money in a holder specifically designed for that use. Coin dealers sell inexpensive holders called "2 by 2s" (because they're 2 inches square), which consist of two pieces of cardboard with a clear window in the center. The coin is placed in between and then the two pieces are stapled together. It's a good idea to keep a supply of 2-by-2s for various denominations on hand.

Do not attempt to clean a coin or repair a piece of paper money. Coin-cleaning methods – particularly home-brewed ones – are often abrasive and will damage a coin rather than improve it. The founders of the California hoard attempted to clean some of the coins they found, and the results lessened coins' value. Likewise, trying to repair a piece of paper money with tape will only lessen its value.

A WORD ABOUT VALUES

If you do find an old coin or piece of paper money, you'll probably want to cash in by selling it to a dealer or another collector. Be advised that the values listed in this book are approximate retail values. These are the approximate prices a collector can expect to pay when purchasing the coin or paper money from a dealer. As a general guide, expect a dealer to offer about half of the value listed here for a particular issue when purchasing coins or paper money from someone who walks in off the street. That's the margin a dealer must work with to be profitable and stay in business.

Well-worn silver coins (pre-1965 dimes, quarters, and half dollars) culled from circulation will probably be worth their silver value only. In those cases, it may be best to wait until you have a significant quantity of silver coins before offering them to a dealer. He may not want to bother with purchasing one silver dime (0.0723 troy ounces of silver).

An educated and sharp eye is all it takes to be a successful picker of coin and paper money. Your finds may not make hobby history, but they may add a few extra dollars to your wallet.

U.S. COIN
PRICING

HALF CENTS

Half cents are much more popular among collectors today than they were in circulation when issued. The small-denomination coins permitted precise dealings in commerce, but they were considered nuisances by those who had to handle them. Demand for half cents in circulation was low, which kept mintages low. In some years, none was struck. In other years, the U.S. Mint didn't allocate any blanks for them and struck them on second-hand merchant tokens instead.

Though not as popularly collected as large cents, half cents today are considered scarce and desirable. Like large cents, half cents are collected by die variety. Rare die combinations can be worth much more than common ones of the same year. Early dates are scarce in better grades. The Classic Head type is much easier to find in better grades.

1825 Classic Head half cent.

Classic Head	VG	VF
1809	80.00	110.00
1810	100.00	500.00
1811	375.00	1,800.00
1825	75.00	110.00
1826	70.00	90.00
1828, 13 stars	70.00	90..00
1828, 12 stars	80.00	175.00
1829	70.00	100.00
1831, original	—	XF 65,000.00
1831, restrike	—	unc. 6,500.00
1832	70.00	85.00
1833	70.00	85.00
1834	70.00	85.00
1835	70.00	85.00
1836, original	—	proof 6,000.00
1836, restrike	—	proof 50,000.00

Braided Hair	PF-60
1840 original	3,250.00
1840 first restrike	3,250.00
1840 second restrike	5,500.00
1841 original	3,250.00
1841 first restrike	3,250.00
1841 second restrike	6,000.00
1842 original	3,250.00
1842 first restrike	3,250.00
1842 second restrike	6,000.00
1843 original	3,250.00
1843 first restrike	3,250.00
1843 second restrike	6,500.00
1844 original	3,250.00
1844 first restrike	3,250.00
1844 second restrike	6,000.00
1845 original	6,000.00
1845 first restrike	3,250.00
1845 second restrike	6,000.00
1846 original	3,250.00
1846 first restrike	3,250.00
1846 second restrike	6,000.00
1847 original	3,250.00
1847 first restrike	3,250.00
1847 second restrike	6,000.00
1848 original	6,000.00
1848 first restrike	3,250.00
1848 second restrike	6,000.00
1849 original, small date	3,250.00
1849 first restrike, small date	3,250.00

1849 Braided Hair half cent.

Braided Hair	VG	VF
1849 large date	75.00	90.00
1850	75.00	90.00
1851	70.00	85.00
1852 original	25,000.00	35,000.00
1852 first restrike	1,500.00	2,600.00

Braided Hair	VG	VF
1852 second restrike	1,500.00	2,600.00
1853	70.00	85.00
1854	70.00	85.00
1855	70.00	85.00
1856	70.00	85.00
1857	75.00	100.00

LARGE CENTS

The large cent resulted from the desire for a decimal coin worth one-hundredth of a dollar and the need for a coin to replace British halfpennies and their imitations, which were common in the Colonies. The large cent was slightly larger than the halfpenny.

Early American coin dies were engraved by hand, so no two were identical. Because of this, collecting large cents by die variety is popular. Rare die combinations are worth more than common ones of the same year.

1828 Coronet large cent.

Coronet	VG	VF
1816	35.00	115.00
1817, 13 obverse stars	35.00	70.00
1817, 15 obverse stars	45.00	165.00
1818	35.00	70.00
1819	35.00	70.00
1820	35.00	70.00
1821	75.00	400.00
1822	35.00	100.00
1823	200.00	700.00
1824	35.00	160.00

Coronet	VG	VF
1825	35.00	110.00
1826	35.00	85.00
1827	35.00	90.00
1828	35.00	80.00
1829	35.00	90.00
1830	30.00	70.00
1831	30.00	70.00
1832	30.00	70.00
1833	30.00	70.00
1834	30.00	70.00
1835	30.00	70.00
1836	30.00	70.00
1837	30.00	70.00
1838	30.00	70.00
1839	35.00	75.00

Braided Hair	VG	VF
1839	35.00	40.00
1840	30.00	35.00
1841	30.00	40.00
1842	30.00	35.00
1843	30.00	35.00
1844	30.00	35.00
1845	30.00	35.00
1846	25.00	35.00
1847	25.00	35.00
1848	30.00	35.00
1849	30.00	35.00
1850	30.00	35.00
1851	25.00	35.00
1852	25.00	35.00
1853	25.00	35.00
1854	25.00	35.00
1855, slanted 5s	55.00	70.00
1855, upright 5s	25.00	35.00
1856, slanted 5	25.00	35.00
1856, upright 5	40.00	55.00
1857, large date	150.00	235.00
1857, small date	110.00	190.00

FLYING EAGLE CENTS

Americans gladly accepted the new, smaller Flying Eagle cents when they were introduced to replace the bulkier large cents. An estimated 2,500 1856-dated Flying Eagle cents were produced before the law authorizing the coin was actually passed. Technically, that makes them patterns, but they are widely listed with the regular production issues of 1857 and 1858, and are commonly considered part of this short-lived series. Collectors should watch for genuine 1857 and 1858 Flying Eagle cents with their dates re-engraved to read 1856.

1858 Flying Eagle cent.

	VG	VF
1856	7,250.00	10,750.00
1857	40.00	45.00
1858	45.00	50.00

INDIAN HEAD CENTS

The Indian Head cent was popularly named for the image of Liberty wearing an American Indian headdress on the obverse. Legend has it that the coin's designer, James B. Longacre, was inspired to create the image when an Indian chief visiting the U.S. Mint took off his headdress and placed it on the head of Longacre's daughter Sarah. It's a charming tale but probably not true. The Indian Head cent's reverse was changed after just one year of production. In 1860, an oak wreath replaced the laurel wreath in the original design and a shield was added at the top. A composition change also occurred in 1864. The original copper-nickel composition was replaced with a bronze composition.

1859 Indian Head cent.

	F	XF
1859	25.00	100.00
1860	20.00	70.00
1861	40.00	95.00
1862	12.50	30.00
1863	11.00	25.00
1864, copper-nickel	35.00	125.00
1864, bronze	25.00	70.00
1865	20.00	45.00
1866	80.00	195.00
1867	110.00	195.00
1868	75.00	180.00
1869	230.00	450.00
1870	225.00	410.00
1871	280.00	420.00
1872	390.00	625.00
1873	65.00	175.00
1874	45.00	110.00
1875	55.00	120.00
1876	75.00	230.00
1877	1,600.00	2,650.00
1878	70.00	245.00
1879	16.50	75.00
1880	6.50	30.00
1881	6.50	20.00
1882	5.00	20.00
1883	4.50	17.50
1884	7.00	30.00
1885	12.00	60.00
1886	20.00	150.00
1887	4.00	20.00
1888	5.00	20.00
1889	3.50	12.00

	F	XF
1890	3.00	10.00
1891	3.25	13.00
1892	4.50	18.50
1893	3.25	10.00
1894	13.00	50.00
1895	3.50	11.00
1896	3.25	13.00
1897	2.75	10.00
1898	2.75	10.00
1899	2.50	10.00
1900	2.50	12.00
1901	2.50	11.00
1902	2.50	10.00
1903	2.50	10.00
1904	2.50	10.00
1905	2.50	9.00
1906	2.50	9.00
1907	2.50	8.50
1908	2.50	9.00
1908-S	100.00	165.00
1909	15.50	18.50
1909-S	720.00	900.00

LINCOLN CENTS

The Lincoln cent was introduced in 1909 to mark the centennial of Abraham Lincoln's birth. Lincoln thus became the first president, and the first real person, to be depicted on a circulating U.S. coin. The coin's original reverse design consistent of two wheat ears framing the words "One Cent." It was changed to a depiction of the Lincoln Memorial in 1959 to mark the 150th anniversary of Lincoln's birth. In 2009, the U.S. Mint struck the Lincoln cent with four different reverses to mark the bicentennial of Lincoln's birth.

The Lincoln cent has also seen several composition changes over the years. In 1943, Lincoln cents were produced in zinc-coated steel to conserve copper for the war effort. Later composition changes were in response to rising prices for copper.

1909-S VDB Lincoln cent.

Wheat Reverse	VF	MS-60
1909 VDB	13.50	25.00
1909-S VDB	1,175.00	1,825.00
1909	4.75	14.50
1909-S	165.00	350.00
1910	1.00	17.50
1910-S	28.00	100.00
1911	2.50	18.50
1911-D	20.00	90.00
1911-S	60.00	175.00
1912	5.50	35.00
1912-D	25.00	165.00
1912-S	40.00	175.00
1913	3.25	35.00
1913-D	11.00	100.00
1913-S	30.00	195.00
1914	6.00	50.00
1914-D	450.00	2,100.00
1914-S	40.00	310.00
1915	18.00	80.00
1915-D	7.00	70.00
1915-S	30.00	190.00
1916	2.50	20.00
1916-D	6.50	90.00
1916-S	9.50	100.00
1917	2.00	18.50
1917-D	5.00	70.00
1917-S	2.50	75.00
1918	1.00	13.50
1918-D	5.50	75.00
1918-S	3.75	70.00
1919	1.00	8.00
1919-D	5.00	60.00

Wheat Reverse	VF	MS-60
1919-S	2.50	50.00
1920	1.25	15.00
1920-D	7.00	70.00
1920-S	2.75	100.00
1921	3.00	40.00
1921-S	6.25	100.00
1922-D	25.00	100.00
1923	1.50	13.50
1923-S	12.50	190.00
1924	1.00	17.50
1924-D	60.00	255.00
1924-S	5.50	110.00
1925	.75	9.50
1925-D	6.25	60.00
1925-S	2.75	85.00
1926	.60	7.50
1926-D	5.25	80.00
1926-S	16.50	140.00
1927	.60	7.50
1927-D	3.50	60.00
1927-S	5.25	65.00
1928	.60	7.50
1928-D	3.75	35.00
1928-S	4.00	70.00
1929	.50	7.00
1929-D	2.75	25.00
1929-S	2.75	20.00
1930	.60	4.00
1930-D	.90	11.00
1930-S	.80	9.50
1931	2.00	20.00
1931-D	8.00	50.00
1931-S	125.00	160.00
1932	3.50	17.50
1932-D	2.85	18.50
1933	2.85	16.50
1933-D	7.50	25.00
1934	.50	9.00
1934-D	1.25	20.00
1935	.50	5.00
1935-D	.50	5.50
1935-S	1.75	11.00

Wheat Reverse	VF	MS-60
1936	.50	5.00
1936-D	.50	4.00
1936-S	.60	5.00
1937	.50	1.75
1937-D	.60	2.75
1937-S	.50	2.70
1938	.50	2.25
1938-D	.60	3.50
1938-S	.70	3.00
1939	.50	1.00
1939-D	.60	3.00
1939-S	.60	2.50
1940	.40	1.00
1940-D	.50	2.00
1940-S	.50	2.50
1941	.40	1.25
1941-D	.50	2.25
1941-S	.50	2.25
1942	.40	.85
1942-D	.35	1.00
1942-S	.85	5.00
1943, steel	.45	1.25
1943-D, steel	.50	1.50
1943-S, steel	.65	4.00

Picker's Tip

The composition of 1943 Lincoln cents was changed from predominately copper to predominately steel to conserve raw materials critical to the war effort. The "war cents" are easily distinguished from other Lincoln cents by their silver-gray color. The 1943 cents are an interesting historical sidebar in the Lincoln series but command only a small premium in typical circulated grades. The Philadelphia, Denver, and San Francisco mints combined struck more than a billion of them.

Wheat Reverse	VF	MS-60
1944	.30	8.00
1944-D	.40	14.00
1944-S	.35	8.00
1945	.40	13.50
1945-D	.40	8.00
1945-S	.40	7.50
1946	.25	13.50
1946-D	.30	10.00
1946-S	.30	13.50
1947	.45	18.50
1947-D	.35	7.50
1947-S	.35	8.00
1948	.35	18.50
1948-D	.40	12.00
1948-S	.40	12.00
1949	.40	15.00
1949-D	.40	15.00
1949-S	.50	10.00
1950	.35	16.50
1950-D	.35	12.50
1950-S	.30	9.00
1951	.40	16.50
1951-D	.30	8.50
1951-S	.40	9.00
1952	.40	16.00
1952-D	.30	8.50
1952-S	.60	12.00
1953	.25	18.00
1953-D	.25	8.50
1953-S	.40	8.00
1954	.25	20.00
1954-D	.25	8.50
1954-S	.25	10.00
1955	.25	9.00
1955-D	.20	8.00
1955-S	.35	7.50
1956	.20	12.00
1956-D	.20	7.00
1957	.20	7.50
1957-D	.20	6.00
1958	.20	9.00
1958-D	.20	7.00

Lincoln Memorial Reverse	MS-65	PF-65
1959	18.00	10.00
1959-D	16.00	—
1960, small date	12.00	18.00
1960, large date	10.00	10.00
1960-D, small date	10.00	—
1960-D, large date	11.00	—
1961	6.50	9.00
1961-D	15.00	—
1962	8.00	8.00
1962-D	14.00	—
1963	10.00	8.00
1963-D	12.00	—
1964	6.50	8.00
1964-D	7.00	—
1965	10.00	—
1966	10.00	—
1967	10.00	—
1968	12.00	—
1968-D	12.00	—
1968-S	8.00	1.00
1969	6.50	—
1969-D	10.00	—
1969-S	8.00	1.10
1970	8.00	—
1970-D	6.00	—
1970-S, small date	75.00	60.00
1970-S, large date	16.00	—
1971	25.00	—
1971-D	5.50	—
1971-S	6.00	1.20
1972	6.00	—
1972-D	10.00	—
1972-S	30.00	1.15
1973	8.00	—
1973-D	11.00	—
1973-S	8.00	.80
1974	12.00	—
1974-D	12.00	—
1974-S	10.00	.75
1975	8.00	—
1975-D	13.50	—
1975-S	—	5.50

Lincoln Memorial Reverse	MS-65	PF-65
1976	18.00	—
1976-D	20.00	—
1976-S	—	5.00
1977	.25	—
1977-D	.25	—
1977-S	—	3.00
1978	.25	—
1978-D	.25	—
1978-S	—	3.50
1979	.25	—
1979-D	.25	—
1979-S	—	4.25
1980	.25	—
1980-D	.25	—
1980-S	—	2.25
1981	.25	—
1981-D	.25	—
1981-S	—	3.50
1982	.25	—
1982-D	.25	—
1982-S	—	3.00
Copper-Plated Zinc Composition	MS-65	PF-65
1982, large date	.50	—
1982, small date	2.00	—
1982-D, large date	.30	—
1982-D, small date	.25	—
1982-S	—	3.00
1983	.25	—
1983-D	.50	—
1983-S	—	4.00
1984	.25	—
1984-D	.75	—
1984-S	—	4.50
1985	.25	—
1985-D	.25	—
1985-S	—	6.00
1986	1.50	—
1986-D	1.25	—
1986-S	—	7.50
1987	.25	—
1987-D	.25	—
1987-S	—	5.00

Copper-Plated Zinc Composition	MS-65	PF-65
1988	.25	—
1988-D	.25	—
1988-S	—	4.00
1989	.25	—
1989-D	.25	—
1989-S	—	6.00
1990	.25	—
1990-D	.25	—
1990-S	—	5.00
1991	.25	—
1991-D	.25	—
1991-S	—	5.00
1992	.25	—
1992-D	.25	—
1992-S	—	5.00
1993	.25	—
1993-D	.25	—
1993-S	—	7.00
1994	.25	—
1994-D	.25	—
1994-S	—	4.00
1995	.25	—
1995-D	.25	—
1995-S	—	9.50
1996	.25	—
1996-D	.25	—
1996-S	—	6.50
1997	.25	—
1997-D	.25	—
1997-S	—	11.50
1998	.25	—
1998-D	.25	—
1998-S	—	9.50
1999	.25	—
1999-D	.25	—
1999-S	—	5.00
2000	.25	—
2000-D	.25	—
2000-S	—	4.00
2001	.25	—
2001-D	.25	—
2001-S	—	4.00

Copper-Plated Zinc Composition	MS-65	PF-65
2002	.25	—
2002-D	.25	—
2002-S	—	4.00
2003	.25	—
2003-D	.25	—
2003-S	—	4.00
2004	.25	—
2004-D	.25	—
2004-S	—	4.00
2005	.25	—
2005-D	.25	—
2005-S	—	4.00
2006	.25	—
2006-D	.25	—
2006-S	—	4.00
2007	1.50	—
2007-D	1.50	—
2007-S	—	4.00
2008	1.50	—
2008-D	1.50	—
2008-S	—	4.00

Log Cabin	MS-65	PF-65
2009-P	1.50	—
2009-P, copper	1.50	—
2009-D	1.50	—
2009-D, copper	1.50	—
2009-S, copper	—	4.00

Lincoln Reading	MS-65	PF-65
2009-P	1.50	—
2009-P, copper	1.50	—
2009-D	1.50	—
2009-D, copper	1.50	—
2009-S, copper	—	4.00

Illinois Old State Capitol	MS-65	PF-65
2009-P	1.50	—
2009-P, copper	1.50	—
2009-D	1.50	—
2009-D, copper	1.50	—
2009-S, copper	—	4.00

U.S. Capitol	MS-65	PF-65
2009-P	1.50	—
2009-P, copper	1.50	—
2009-D	1.50	—
2009-D, copper	1.50	—
2009-S, copper	—	4.00

Union Shield Reverse	MS-65	PF-65
2010	1.50	—
2010-D	1.50	—
2010-S	—	4.00
2011-P	1.50	—
2011-D	1.50	—
2011-S	—	4.00
2012	1.50	—
2012-D	1.50	—
2012-S	—	4.00

TWO CENTS

The two-cent piece is famous for being the first U.S. coin to carry the motto "In God We Trust." It was introduced in response to a shortage of small change during the Civil War.

	F	XF
1864, small motto	285.00	650.00
1864, large motto	20.00	—
1865	20.00	45.00
1866	20.00	45.00
1867	35.00	65.00
1868	35.00	65.00
1869	40.00	80.00
1870	60.00	135.00
1871	70.00	150.00
1872	700.00	1,200
1873, closed 3	—	proof 1,750
1873, open 3	—	proof 1,875

SILVER THREE CENTS

Silver three-cent coins were issued to facilitate purchases of three-cent postage stamps. In terms of size, they are the smallest coins in U.S. history and are also thin. They didn't strike up well, so today it's difficult to find fully struck examples with no weak spots in the design even in higher grades. The Type 1 design has no outlines in the star. The Type 2 design has three lines outlining the star. The Type 3 design has two lines outlining the star.

1851 Type 1 silver three-cent piece.

Type 1	F	XF
1851	50.00	70.00
1851-O	60.00	160.00
1852	50.00	70.00
1853	50.00	70.00

1856 Type 2 silver three-cent piece.

Type 2	F	XF
1854	50.00	115.00
1855	75.00	200.00
1856	55.00	120.00
1857	55.00	115.00
1858	50.00	120.00

1862 Type 3 silver three-cent piece.

Type 3	F	XF
1859	55.00	85.00
1860	55.00	85.00
1861	55.00	85.00
1862	60.00	90.00
1863	450.00	520.00
1864	450.00	520.00
1865	550.00	665.00
1866	450.00	520.00
1867	575.00	675.00
1868	585.00	690.00
1869	585.00	690.00
1870	525.00	665.00
1871	535.00	670.00
1872	550.00	690.00

NICKEL THREE CENTS

Though produced concurrently for several years, the larger nickel three-cent was intended to replace the smaller, more fragile silver three-cent. Also, the nickel alloy saved the new coins from Civil War-era silver hoarders.

1885 nickel three-cent.

	F	XF
1865	17.50	35.00
1866	17.50	35.00
1867	17.50	35.00
1868	17.50	35.00
1869	19.50	40.00
1870	20.00	40.00
1871	25.00	45.00
1872	25.00	45.00
1873	20.00	40.00
1874	20.00	40.00
1875	30.00	45.00
1876	25.00	50.00
1877	—	proof 1,300.00
1878	—	proof 800.00
1879	95.00	115.00
1880	130.00	185.00
1881	20.00	40.00
1882	180.00	300.00
1883	260.00	375.00
1884	550.00	645.00
1885	645.00	745.00
1886	—	proof 385.00
1887	400.00	455.00
1888	70.00	100.00
1889	140.00	220.00

SEATED LIBERTY HALF DIMES

The half dime was one of the denominations originally authorized by the Mint Act of 1792. Half-dime
designs through the years emulated those on the larger
dime. Half dimes were thin and susceptible to bending
and dents in circulation. In the Seated Liberty half-dime
series, drapery was added to Liberty's left elbow in 1840.
The arrows at date in 1853 signaled a reduction in the
coin's weight, from 1.34 grams to 1.24 grams, and a reduction in its silver content, from 0.0388 troy ounces to
0.0362 troy ounces. The arrows were removed from the
design in 1856.

1838-O Seated Liberty half dime, no stars on obverse.

No Stars on Obverse	F	XF
1837, small date	75.00	220.00
1837, large date	80.00	235.00
1838-O	250.00	975.00

1849-O Seated Liberty half dime, stars on obverse.

Stars on Obverse	F	XF
1838, large stars	30.00	90.00
1838, small stars	45.00	190.00
1839	30.00	95.00
1839-O	35.00	90.00
1840, no drapery	30.00	80.00
1840-O, no drapery	40.00	140.00
1840, with drapery	75.00	210.00
1840-O, with drapery	115.00	650.00
1841	25.00	60.00
1841-O	30.00	125.00
1842	25.00	55.00
1842-O	75.00	550.00
1843	25.00	55.00
1844	25.00	60.00
1844-O	210.00	1,300.00
1845	25.00	60.00
1846	850.00	2,475.00
1847	25.00	55.00
1848, medium date	25.00	65.00
1848 large date	50.00	145.00
1848-O	35.00	135.00
1849	30.00	65.00
1849-O	95.00	540.00
1850	25.00	60.00
1850-O	35.00	125.00
1851	25.00	60.00
1851-O	25.00	110.00

Stars on Obverse	F	XF
1852	25.00	60.00
1852-O	80.00	275.00
1853	90.00	300.00
1853-O	450.00	1,800.00

1854 Seated Liberty half dime, arrows at date.

Arrows at Date	F	XF
1853	25.00	60.00
1853-O	30.00	65.00
1854	25.00	60.00
1854-O	35.00	90.00
1855	25.00	60.00
1855-O	40.00	140.00

1856 Seated Liberty half dime, arrows at date removed.

Arrows at Date Removed	F	XF
1856	25.00	50.00
1856-O	25.00	95.00
1857	25.00	50.00
1857-O	25.00	60.00
1858	25.00	50.00
1858-O	25.00	70.00
1859	25.00	55.00
1859-O	25.00	130.00

1863-S Seated Liberty half dime, with legend on obverse.

Obverse Legend	F	XF
1860	25.00	45.00
1860-O	25.00	50.00
1861	20.00	45.00
1862	35.00	65.00
1863	300.00	485.00
1863-S	70.00	165.00

Obverse Legend	F	XF
1864	575.00	950.00
1864-S	115.00	250.00
1865	575.00	950.00
1865-S	60.00	145.00
1866	550.00	875.00
1866-S	60.00	145.00
1867	775.00	1,100.00
1867-S	60.00	150.00
1868	190.00	300.00
1868-S	35.00	60.00
1869	35.00	60.00
1869-S	30.00	55.00
1870	30.00	55.00
1870-S	—	one known
1871	20.00	45.00
1871-S	45.00	90.00
1872	20.00	45.00
1872-S	25.00	45.00
1873	20.00	45.00
1873-S	30.00	60.00

LIBERTY NICKELS

The Liberty nickel was originally struck with just a large Roman-numeral "V" on its reverse to indicate its value. At the time, some unscrupulous individuals gold plated the new nickels and passed them off as $5 coins. Thus, later in its first year of production, the word "Cents" was added to its reverse.

It is believed that the 1913 Liberty nickels were the unauthorized strikings of a U.S. Mint employee. Today, they are among numismatics' great rarities. All six known examples are accounted for in either private hands or museum holdings.

	F	XF
1883, without "Cents"	8.50	9.25
1883, with "Cents"	40.00	85.00
1884	40.00	90.00
1885	875.00	1,350.00

1907 Liberty nickel.

	F	XF
1886	400.00	685.00
1887	30.00	80.00
1888	70.00	185.00
1889	30.00	75.00
1890	25.00	70.00
1891	20.00	60.00
1892	25.00	65.00
1893	25.00	60.00
1894	100.00	230.00
1895	25.00	65.00
1896	40.00	100.00
1897	12.50	45.00
1898	11.00	40.00
1899	8.50	35.00
1900	8.50	35.00
1901	7.00	35.00
1902	4.00	30.00
1903	4.75	30.00
1904	4.75	30.00
1905	4.00	30.00
1906	4.00	30.00
1907	4.00	30.00
1908	4.00	30.00
1909	4.50	35.00
1910	4.00	30.00
1911	4.00	30.00
1912	4.00	30.00
1912-D	11.50	70.00
1912-S	220.00	810.00
1913	—	6 known

BUFFALO NICKELS

The Buffalo nickel, also and more appropriately called the Indian Head nickel, was a refreshing departure from previous coin designs. Noted sculptor James Earle Fraser designed the coin. It was long believed that three different Native Americans posed for the obverse portrait, but that theory has been questioned recently.

The original reverse, depicting an American bison standing on a mound, was changed because the words "Five Cents" were in such high relief that they wore off quickly. The second reverse has the denomination in a recess below a plane on which the bison stands. The date is also in high relief and, as a result, is usually worn off on coins grading below very good. "Dateless" Buffalo nickels have little value.

1913 Buffalo nickel.

	F	MS-60
1913 mound	15.00	35.00
1913-D mound	20.00	65.00
1913-S mound	50.00	125.00
1913 line	13.00	35.00
1913-D line	180.00	285.00
1913-S line	420.00	885.00
1914	20.00	45.00
1914-D	165.00	475.00
1914-S	45.00	165.00
1915	7.75	50.00
1915-D	40.00	235.00
1915-S	100.00	625.00

	F	MS-60
1916	7.00	45.00
1916-D	30.00	165.00
1916-S	25.00	185.00
1917	8.75	60.00
1917-D	55.00	345.00
1917-S	80.00	400.00
1918	8.00	100.00
1918-D	65.00	430.00
1918-S	55.00	500.00
1919	4.00	60.00
1919-D	65.00	570.00
1919-S	50.00	540.00
1920	3.25	60.00
1920-D	35.00	575.00
1920-S	30.00	525.00
1921	8.50	125.00
1921-S	180.00	1,575.00
1923	4.25	60.00
1923-S	25.00	625.00
1924	4.50	75.00
1924-D	30.00	375.00
1924-S	95.00	2,300.00
1925	3.75	40.00
1925-D	40.00	375.00
1925-S	17.50	425.00
1926	3.00	30.00
1926-D	30.00	335.00
1926-S	100.00	4,950.00
1927	2.50	35.00
1927-D	7.00	155.00
1927-S	6.00	490.00
1928	2.50	30.00
1928-D	3.75	55.00
1928-S	3.00	225.00
1929	2.50	35.00
1929-D	3.00	60.00
1929-S	2.25	50.00
1930	2.50	35.00
1930-S	3.00	65.00
1931-S	17.00	60.00
1934	2.50	45.00

	F	MS-60
1934-D	4.75	80.00
1935	2.25	20.00
1935-D	3.00	70.00
1935-S	2.50	50.00
1936	2.25	14.50
1936-D	2.75	35.00
1936-S	2.50	35.00
1937	2.25	14.50
1937-D	2.50	30.00
1937-D, three-legged	725.00	2,375.00
1937-S	2.50	25.00
1938-D	4.00	25.00

JEFFERSON NICKELS

The Jefferson nickel was the first circulating U.S. coin to be designed by public contest. Felix Schlag won $1,000 for his design featuring Thomas Jefferson on the obverse and his home, Monticello, on the reverse. Schlag's initials were added to the design in 1966.

The steps leading up to Monticello on the reverse are a key to evaluating the coin. They don't always strike up completely, so Jefferson nickels with fully struck steps command a premium.

During World War II, nickel was needed for the war effort, so from mid-1942 through 1945, "nickels" were struck in an unusual alloy of 56-percent copper, 35-percent silver, and 9-percent manganese. The "war nickels" have a large mint mark over the dome of Monticello on the reverse.

Congress authorized new nickel designs for 2004 and 2005 to commemorate the bicentennial of Lewis and Clark's exploration of the American West following the Louisiana Purchase. As president, Jefferson authorized the mission to find the "most direct and practicable water communication across this continent for the purpose of commerce." For 2006, an image of Jefferson based on a Rembrandt Peale portrait from 1800 was used on the obverse.

1939 Jefferson nickel.

	F	MS-60
1938	.75	7.50
1938-D	1.25	4.00
1938-S	2.00	5.25
1939	.20	1.75
1939-D	5.00	55.00
1939-S	.60	17.00
1940	.20	1.00
1940-D	.20	1.50
1940-S	.40	4.50
1941	—	.75
1941-D	.30	2.25
1941-S	.40	5.00
1942	—	5.00
1942-D	3.00	40.00

The mintmark on wartime-composition nickels appears above the dome of Monticello on the reverse.

Wartime Composition	VF	MS-60
1942-P	2.50	9.00
1942-S	2.50	11.00
1943-P	2.50	5.00
1943-D	2.50	4.00
1943-S	2.50	6.75
1944-P	2.50	14.00
1944-D	2.50	12.00
1944-S	2.50	9.50
1945-P	2.50	6.00
1945-D	2.50	5.50
1945-S	2.50	5.00

Pre-War Composition Resumed	XF	MS-65
1946	.25	20.00
1946-D	.35	16.00
1946-S	.40	17.00
1947	.25	18.00
1947-D	.30	15.00
1947-S	.25	15.00
1948	.25	16.00
1948-D	.35	14.00
1948-S	.50	14.00
1949	.30	18.00
1949-D	.40	12.00
1949-S	1.00	10.00
1950	.75	12.00
1950-D	10.00	20.00
1951	.50	18.00
1951-D	.50	14.00
1951-S	1.00	18.50
1952	.25	17.00
1952-D	.50	18.00
1952-S	.25	18.00
1953	.25	9.00
1953-D	.25	16.00
1953-S	.25	20.00
1954	.20	9.00
1954-D	.20	10.00
1954-S	.20	16.00
1955	.45	6.50
1955-D	.15	16.00
1956	.15	16.00
1956-D	.15	16.00
1957	.15	12.00
1957-D	.15	12.00
1958	.20	30.00
1958-D	.15	13.00
1959	—	8.00
1959-D	—	5.50
1960	—	6.00
1960-D	—	20.00
1961	—	6.00
1961-D	—	20.00
1962	—	5.00
1962-D	—	.75

Pre-War Composition Resumed	XF	MS-65
1963	—	.55
1963-D	—	.55
1964	—	.55
1964-D	—	.50
1965	—	.50
1966	—	.50
1967	—	.50
1968-D	—	4.50
1968-S	—	.50
1969-D	—	.50
1969-S	—	.50
1970-D	—	.50
1970-S	—	8.00
1971	—	2.00
1971-D	—	.50
1971-S	—	proof 2.00
1972	—	.50
1972-D	—	.50
1972-S	—	proof 2.00
1973	—	.50
1973-D	—	.50
1973-S	—	proof 1.75
1974	—	.50
1974-D	—	.50
1974-S	—	proof 2.00
1975	—	.75
1975-D	—	.50
1975-S	—	proof 2.25
1976	—	.75
1976-D	—	.60
1976-S	—	proof 3.00
1977	—	.40
1977-D	—	.55
1977-S	—	proof 1.75
1978	—	.40
1978-D	—	.40
1978-S	—	proof 1.75
1979	—	.40
1979-D	—	.40
1979-S	—	proof 1.50
1980-P	—	6.00
1980-D	—	.40

Pre-War Composition Resumed	XF	MS-65
1980-S	—	proof 1.50
1981-P	—	.40
1981-D	—	.40
1981-S	—	proof 2.00
1982-P	—	12.50
1982-D	—	3.50
1982-S	—	proof 3.50
1983-P	—	4.00
1983-D	—	2.50
1983-S	—	proof 4.00
1984-P	—	3.00
1984-D	—	.85
1984-S	—	proof 5.00
1985-P	—	.75
1985-D	—	.75
1985-S	—	proof 4.00
1986-P	—	1.00
1986-D	—	2.00
1986-S	—	proof 7.00
1987-P	—	.75
1987-D	—	.75
1987-S	—	proof 3.50
1988-P	—	.75
1988-D	—	.75
1988-S	—	proof 6.50
1989-P	—	.75
1989-D	—	.75
1989-S	—	proof 5.50
1990-P	—	.75
1990-D	—	.75
1990-S	—	proof 5.50
1991-P	—	.75
1991-D	—	.75
1991-S	—	proof 5.00
1992-P	—	2.00
1992-D	—	.75
1992-S	—	proof 4.00
1993-P	—	.75
1993-D	—	.75
1993-S	—	proof 4.50
1994-P	—	.75
1994-D	—	.75

Pre-War Composition Resumed	XF	MS-65
1994-S	—	proof 4.00
1995-P	—	.75
1995-D	—	.85
1995-S	—	proof 4.00
1996-P	—	.75
1996-D	—	.75
1996-S	—	proof 4.00
1997-P	—	.75
1997-D	—	2.00
1997-S		proof 5.00
1998-P	—	.80
1998-D	—	.80
1998-S		proof 4.50
1999-P	—	.80
1999-D	—	.80
1999-S		proof 3.50
2000-P	—	.80
2000-D	—	.80
2000-S		proof 2.00
2001-P	—	.50
2001-D	—	.50
2001-S		proof 4.00
2002-P	—	.50
2002-D	—	.50
2002-S		proof 2.00
2003-P	—	.50
2003-D	—	.50
2003-S		proof 2.00

Peace Medal	MS-65	PF-65
2004-P	1.50	—
2004-D	1.50	—
2004-S	—	10.00

Keelboat	MS-65	PF-65
2004-P	1.50	—
2004-D	1.50	—
2004-S	—	10.00

Bison	MS-65	PF-65
2005-P	1.50	—
2005-D	1.50	—
2005-S	—	6.50

"Ocean in view!"	MS-65	PF-65
2005-P	1.25	—
2005-D	1.25	—
2005-S	—	5.50

2011-D Jefferson nickel with new portrait.

New Jefferson Portrait	MS-65	PF-65
2006-P	2.50	—
2006-P, satin finish	4.00	—
2006-D	2.50	—
2006-D, satin finish	4.00	—
2006-S	—	5.00
2007-P	2.50	—
2007-P, satin finish	4.00	—
2007-D	2.50	—
2007-D, satin finish	4.00	—
2007-S	—	4.00
2008-P	2.50	—
2008-P, satin finish	4.00	—
2008-D	2.50	—
2008-D, satin finish	4.00	—
2008-S	—	4.00
2009-P	2.50	—
2009-P, satin finish	4.00	—
2009-D	2.50	—
2009-D, satin finish	4.00	—
2009-S	—	3.00
2010-P	2.50	—

New Jefferson Portrait	MS-65	PF-65
2010-P satin finish	4.00	—
2010-D	2.50	—
2010-D satin finish	4.00	—
2010-S	—	3.00
2011-P	2.50	—
2011-D	2.50	—
2011-S	—	3.00
2012-P	2.50	—
2012-D	2.50	—
2012-S	—	3.00

SEATED LIBERTY DIMES

Christian Gobrecht's Seated Liberty design first appeared on the dollar and was later adapted for the lower denominations. The Seated Liberty dime underwent a number of modifications in design and specifications during its long run. In some cases, a design tweak indicated a change in specifications. In 1840, drapery was added to Liberty's left elbow.

1837 Seated Liberty dime, no stars on obverse.

No Stars on Obverse	VG	VF
1837	55.00	250.00
1838-O	60.00	375.00

1844 Seated Liberty dime with stars on obverse.

Stars on Obverse	VG	VF
1838, small stars	40.00	85.00
1838, large stars	25.00	45.00
1839	25.00	40.00
1839-O	30.00	140.00

Stars on Obverse	VG	VF
1840, no drapery	25.00	40.00
1840-O, no drapery	30.00	60.00
1840, with drapery	50.00	175.00
1841	20.00	30.00
1841-O	30.00	40.00
1842	18.00	30.00
1842-O	30.00	75.00
1843	18.00	30.00
1843-O	75.00	300.00
1844	300.00	600.00
1845	18.00	30.00
1845-O	50.00	225.00
1846	250.00	575.00
1847	30.00	70.00
1848	25.00	50.00
1849	20.00	35.00
1849-O	35.00	125.00
1850	20.00	35.00
1850-O	30.00	75.00
1851	20.00	30.00
1851-O	35.00	85.00
1852	18.00	25.00
1852-O	35.00	145.00
1853	145.00	300.00

1853 Seated Liberty dime with arrows at date.

Arrows at Date	VG	VF
1853	18.00	25.00
1853-O	20.00	45.00
1854	18.00	22.00
1854-O	20.00	25.00
1855	18.00	20.00
Arrows at Date Removed	**VG**	**VF**
1856	17.00	20.00
1856-O	20.00	30.00
1856-S	185.00	575.00
1857	17.00	20.00
1857-O	18.00	25.00

1856 Seated Liberty dime
with arrows at date removed.

Arrows at Date Removed	VG	VF
1858	17.00	20.00
1858-O	25.00	85.00
1858-S	200.00	475.00
1859	20.00	40.00
1859-O	20.00	40.00
1859-S	175.00	600.00
1860-S	55.00	145.00

1865 Seated Liberty dime
with legend on obverse.

Obverse Legend	VG	VF
1860	20.00	30.00
1860-O	600.00	1,950.00
1861	18.00	25.00
1861-S	90.00	200.00
1862	20.00	25.00
1862-S	60.00	175.00
1863	500.00	900.00
1863-S	55.00	145.00
1864	500.00	800.00
1864-S	45.00	120.00
1865	575.00	875.00
1865-S	55.00	200.00
1866	600.00	950.00
1866-S	65.00	150.00
1867	700.00	1,100.00
1867-S	80.00	200.00
1868	30.00	50.00
1868-S	40.00	115.00
1869	35.00	110.00
1869-S	30.00	55.00
1870	20.00	40.00
1870-S	375.00	650.00
1871	18.00	30.00

Obverse Legend	VG	VF
1871-CC	3,500.00	9,500.00
1871-S	55.00	135.00
1872	16.50	20.00
1872-S	65.00	150.00
1872-CC	1,250.00	3,000.00
1873, closed 3	18.00	25.00
1873, open 3	35.00	90.00
1873-CC, rare	—	—

1873-CC Seated Liberty dime with arrows at date.

Arrows at Date	VG	VF
1873	20.00	60.00
1873-CC	2,850.00	9,500.00
1873-S	30.00	80.00
1874	19.00	60.00
1874-CC	7,000.00	18,500.00
1874-S	60.00	150.00

1879 Seated Liberty dime with arrows at date removed.

Arrows at Date Removed	VG	VF
1875	17.50	20.00
1875-CC	35.00	60.00
1875-S, mint mark in wreath	25.00	40.00
1875-S, mint mark under wreath	18.00	20.00
1876	20.00	30.00
1876-CC	35.00	60.00
1876-S	17.50	25.00
1877	20.00	30.00
1877-CC	35.00	60.00
1877-S	16.50	25.00
1878	16.50	25.00
1878-CC	90.00	225.00
1879	310.00	500.00

Arrows at Date Removed	VG	VF
1880	275.00	425.00
1881	300.00	450.00
1882	16.00	20.00
1883	16.00	20.00
1884	16.00	20.00
1884-S	35.00	55.00
1885	16.00	20.00
1885-S	575.00	1,400.00
1886	16.50	20.00
1886-S	45.00	125.00
1887	16.00	20.00
1887-S	16.00	20.00
1888	16.00	20.00
1888-S	16.00	25.00
1889	16.00	20.00
1889-S	18.00	45.00
1890	16.00	20.00
1890-S	16.00	45.00
1891	16.00	20.00
1891-O	17.50	25.00
1891-S	17.00	20.00

BARBER DIMES

The dime, quarter, and half dollar were all revised in 1892 to depict a right-facing portrait of Liberty designed by U.S. Mint Chief Engraver Charles Barber, for whom they have been popularly named.

	F	XF
1892	16.00	30.00
1892-O	35.00	75.00
1892-S	210.00	285.00
1893	20.00	45.00
1893-O	135.00	190.00
1893-S	40.00	85.00
1894	125.00	190.00
1894-O	215.00	425.00
1894-S, rare	30.00	40.00
1895	355.00	565.00

1898-S Barber dime.

	F	XF
1895-O	900.00	2,500.00
1895-S	135.00	240.00
1896	55.00	100.00
1896-O	300.00	465.00
1896-S	310.00	385.00
1897	8.00	30.00
1897-O	290.00	480.00
1897-S	100.00	185.00
1898	7.50	30.00
1898-O	90.00	200.00
1898-S	35.00	80.00
1899	7.50	25.00
1899-O	75.00	150.00
1899-S	35.00	45.00
1900	7.00	25.00
1900-O	115.00	225.00
1900-S	12.50	30.00
1901	6.50	30.00
1901-O	16.00	70.00
1901-S	360.00	520.00
1902	6.25	25.00
1902-O	15.00	65.00
1902-S	60.00	135.00
1903	6.25	25.00
1903-O	13.50	50.00
1903-S	350.00	750.00
1904	7.00	25.00
1904-S	165.00	335.00
1905	6.75	25.00

	F	XF
1905-O	35.00	90.00
1905-S	9.00	45.00
1906	4.50	20.00
1906-D	7.00	35.00
1906-O	50.00	100.00
1906-S	12.50	45.00
1907	4.25	20.00
1907-D	8.75	45.00
1907-O	35.00	65.00
1907-S	16.00	65.00
1908	4.25	20.00
1908-D	5.75	30.00
1908-O	45.00	90.00
1908-S	11.50	45.00
1909	4.25	20.00
1909-D	60.00	135.00
1909-O	12.50	50.00
1909-S	90.00	180.00
1910	4.00	20.00
1910-D	8.50	50.00
1910-S	50.00	110.00
1911	4.00	20.00
1911-D	4.00	20.00
1911-S	8.50	40.00
1912	4.00	20.00
1912-D	4.00	20.00
1912-S	5.50	35.00
1913	4.00	20.00
1913-S	120.00	240.00
1914	4.00	20.00
1914-D	4.00	20.00
1914-S	8.00	40.00
1915	4.00	20.00
1915-S	35.00	65.00
1916	4.00	20.00
1916-S	5.00	25.00

MERCURY DIMES

The common name Mercury for this dime is a misnomer. Designed by Adolph Weinman, it actually depicts Liberty wearing a winged cap, representing freedom of thought, rather than the Roman god Mercury. The reverse depicts the ancient Roman fasces, a symbol of authority that is part of the U.S. Senate's official seal.

The horizontal bands tying the fasces together do not always strike up distinctly from each other. Mercury dimes with "fully split bands" often command a premium.

1916-D Mercury dime.

	VF	MS-60
1916	7.00	30.00
1916-D	3,950.00	13,200.00
1916-S	15.00	45.00
1917	5.50	30.00
1917-D	25.00	120.00
1917-S	7.50	60.00
1918	12.00	70.00
1918-D	13.00	100.00
1918-S	11.00	90.00
1919	5.50	35.00
1919-D	30.00	175.00
1919-S	20.00	175.00
1920	4.50	30.00
1920-D	9.00	110.00
1920-S	9.00	110.00
1921	245.00	1,150.00
1921-D	365.00	1,250.00
1923	4.50	30.00
1923-S	20.00	155.00
1924	4.50	40.00
1924-D	25.00	165.00
1924-S	12.00	185.00

	VF	MS-60
1925	5.50	30.00
1925-D	45.00	335.00
1925-S	18.50	180.00
1926	4.00	25.00
1926-D	12.00	125.00
1926-S	65.00	850.00
1927	4.50	25.00
1927-D	25.00	165.00
1927-S	11.00	270.00
1928	4.50	30.00
1928-D	25.00	165.00
1928-S	6.50	140.00
1929	4.50	20.00
1929-D	8.00	30.00
1929-S	5.00	35.00
1930	2.50	25.00
1930-S	6.50	80.00
1931	4.75	35.00
1931-D	20.00	100.00
1931-S	11.00	100.00
1934	2.50	30.00
1934-D	7.50	50.00
1935	2.50	10.00
1935-D	6.50	40.00
1935-S	3.50	25.00
1936	2.50	9.00
1936-D	4.25	30.00
1936-S	3.00	20.00
1937	2.50	8.00
1937-D	3.00	20.00
1937-S	3.00	20.00
1938	2.50	13.50
1938-D	5.00	18.50
1938-S	3.00	20.00
1939	2.50	9.00
1939-D	2.50	7.50
1939-S	3.00	25.00
1940	2.50	6.00
1940-D	2.50	8.00
1940-S	2.50	8.50
1941	2.50	6.00
1941-D	2.50	8.00

	VF	MS-60
1941-S	2.50	7.00
1942	2.50	6.00
1942-D	2.50	8.00
1942-S	2.50	10.00
1943	2.50	6.00
1943-D	2.50	8.00
1943-S	2.50	9.50
1944	2.50	6.00
1944-D	2.50	7.50
1944-S	2.50	7.50
1945	2.50	6.00
1945-D	2.50	6.50
1945-S	2.50	7.00

ROOSEVELT DIMES

The Roosevelt dime was introduced as a tribute to the late President Franklin D. Roosevelt and was designed by U.S. Mint Chief Engraver John R. Sinnock. Calls for Roosevelt to be honored on a coin came soon after his death on April 12, 1945. Congressional approval is required to change any coin design that has been used for less than 25 years. At the time of Roosevelt's death, the Lincoln cent, Mercury dime, and Walking Liberty half dollar were eligible for redesign. The dime was chosen because the March of Dimes was a fund-raising campaign for the National Foundation for Infantile Paralysis, which Roosevelt established in 1938. Roosevelt suffered from the disease, commonly called polio.

1964 Roosevelt dime.

	MS-60	MS-65
1946	4.00	14.50
1946-D	4.00	13.50
1946-S	4.00	18.50
1947	3.75	15.00
1947-D	4.50	16.00
1947-S	3.75	15.00
1948	3.75	14.00
1948-D	5.00	15.00
1948-S	4.50	17.00
1949	16.00	65.00
1949-D	9.00	25.00
1949-S	35.00	65.00
1950	7.00	30.00
1950-D	3.75	15.00
1950-S	25.00	70.00
1951	4.00	11.00
1951-D	4.00	11.00
1951-S	10.00	35.00
1952	4.00	20.00
1952-D	4.00	11.00
1952-S	5.50	16.00
1953	4.00	12.00
1953-D	4.25	11.00
1953-S	5.50	12.50
1954	4.00	10.00
1954-D	4.00	10.00
1954-S	4.00	10.00
1955	4.00	8.50
1955-D	4.00	8.50
1955-S	4.00	8.00
1956	4.00	9.50
1956-D	4.00	9.00
1957	4.00	8.50
1957-D	4.00	7.50
1958	4.00	11.00
1958-D	4.00	10.00
1959	4.00	8.00
1959-D	4.00	8.50
1960	3.50	8.50
1960-D	4.00	7.50
1961	4.00	8.00
1961-D	4.00	6.50

	MS-60	MS-65
1962	4.00	6.50
1962-D	4.00	7.00
1963	4.00	7.50
1963-D	4.00	7.00
1964	4.00	7.50
1964-D	4.00	7.00

Clad Composition	MS-65	PF-65
1965	6.00	—
1966	6.50	—
1967	7.00	—
1968	6.50	—
1968-D	6.50	—
1968-S	—	4.00
1969	7.00	—
1969-D	6.00	—
1969-S	—	4.00
1970	5.50	—
1970-D	5.00	—
1970-S	—	4.00
1971	10.00	—
1971-D	8.00	—
1971-S	—	4.00
1972	7.50	—
1972-D	8.50	—
1972-S	—	4.00
1973	6.00	—
1973-D	5.50	—
1973-S	—	4.00
1974	5.50	—
1974-D	4.50	—
1974-S	—	4.00
1975	4.50	—
1975-D	4.50	—
1975-S	—	4.00
1976	4.50	—

1968 Roosevelt dime.

Clad Composition	MS-65	PF-65
1976-D	4.50	—
1976-S	—	4.00
1977	4.50	—
1977-D	8.00	—
1977-S	—	4.00
1978	5.00	—
1978-D	4.50	—
1978-S	—	4.00
1979	5.50	—
1979-D	5.00	—
1979-S	—	2.00
1980-P	6.00	—
1980-D	5.00	—
1980-S	—	4.00
1981-P	4.00	—
1981-D	4.00	—
1981-S	—	4.00
1982-P	8.50	—
1982-D	3.25	—
1982-S	—	4.00
1983-P	6.00	—
1983-D	4.00	—
1983-S	—	4.00
1984-P	4.00	—
1984-D	3.50	—
1984-S	—	4.00
1985-P	5.00	—
1985-D	3.50	—
1985-S	—	4.00
1986-P	3.50	—
1986-D	3.50	—
1986-S	—	4.00
1987-P	4.50	—
1987-D	4.50	—
1987-S	—	4.00
1988-P	5.50	—
1988-D	5.50	—
1988-S	—	3.00
1989-P	4.00	—
1989-D	5.00	—
1989-S	—	4.00
1990-P	4.50	—

Clad Composition	MS-65	PF-65
1990-D	5.50	—
1990-S	—	4.00
1991-P	5.00	—
1991-D	5.00	—
1991-S	—	3.00
1992-P	4.50	—
1992-D	4.50	—
1992-S	—	4.00
1992-S silver	—	5.00
1993-P	3.50	—
1993-D	4.50	—
1993-S	—	7.00
1993-S silver	—	9.00
1994-P	4.00	—
1994-D	5.50	—
1994-S	—	5.00
1994-S silver	—	9.00
1995-P	4.00	—
1995-D	4.50	—
1995-S	—	20.00
1995-S silver	—	12.00
1996-P	3.00	—
1996-D	5.00	—
1996-W	25.00	—
1996-S	—	3.50
1996-S silver	—	8.00
1997-P	4.00	—
1997-D	3.00	—
1997-S	—	14.00
1997-S silver	—	14.00
1998-P	2.75	—
1998-D	2.75	—
1998-S	—	4.00
1998-S silver	—	8.00
1999-P	2.75	—
1999-D	2.75	—
1999-S	—	4.00
1999-S silver	—	8.00
2000-P	2.75	—
2000-D	2.75	—
2000-S	—	1.00
2000-S silver	—	5.50

Clad Composition	MS-65	PF-65
2001-P	2.75	—
2001-D	2.75	—
2001-S	—	3.75
2001-S silver	—	5.00
2002-P	2.75	—
2002-D	3.00	—
2002-S	—	2.50
2002-S silver	—	5.00
2003-P	3.00	—
2003-D	3.00	—
2003-S	—	2.50
2003-S silver	—	4.75
2004-P	3.00	—
2004-D	3.00	—
2004-S	—	4.75
2004-S silver	—	5.00
2005-P	2.75	—
2005-D	2.75	—
2005-S	—	2.50
2005-S silver	—	5.00
2006-P	2.50	—
2006-D	2.50	—
2006-S	—	2.50
2006-S silver	—	4.50
2007-P	2.00	—
2007-D	2.00	—
2007-S	—	2.50
2007-S silver	—	6.00
2008-P	1.25	—
2008-D	1.25	—
2008-S	—	2.50
2008-S silver	—	6.50
2009-P	1.25	—
2009-D	1.25	—
2009-S	—	2.50
2009-S silver	—	6.75
2010-P	4.00	—
2010-D	4.00	—
2010-S	—	2.50
2010-S silver	—	6.75
2011-P	4.00	—
2011-D	4.00	—

Clad Composition	MS-65	PF-65
2011-S	—	2.50
2011-S silver	—	6.75
2012-P	4.00	—
2012-D	4.00	—
2012-S	—	2.50
2012-S silver	—	6.75

TWENTY CENTS

When designing the 20-cent piece, U.S. Mint officials were concerned that the public would confuse it with the quarter because of the similarity in size. To give it a distinctive look, the eagle on the reverse faces to its left rather than its right, as on the quarter; the word "Liberty" on the obverse shield is in relief rather than incuse; and the 20-cent coin's edge is plain rather than reeded. The changes weren't enough, however, and circulation production of the coin ended after only two years.

Most of the 1876-CC circulation-production coins were not released and were melted by the Mint. Only one is known to exist today. Only collector proofs were struck in 1877 and 1878.

1876 20-cent piece.

	VG	VF
1875	210.00	325.00
1875-S	110.00	175.00
1875-CC	385.00	600.00
1876	225.00	350.00
1876-CC	—	proof 60,000.00
1877	—	proof 3,500.00
1878	—	proof 2,800.00

SEATED LIBERTY QUARTERS

Christian Gobrecht's Seated Liberty design first appeared on the dollar and was later adapted for the lower denominations. The Seated Liberty quarter underwent a number of modifications in design and specifications during its long run. In some cases, a design tweak indicated a change in specifications. In 1840, drapery was added to Liberty's left elbow.

1847 Seated Liberty quarter.

	VG	VF
1838	40.00	95.00
1839	45.00	90.00
1840-O, no drapery	55.00	135.00
1840, with drapery	35.00	100.00
1840-O, with drapery	55.00	200.00
1841	75.00	190.00
1841-O	35.00	85.00
1842	140.00	325.00
1842-O, small date	1,000.00	2,650.00
1842-O, large date	45.00	95.00
1843	30.00	45.00
1843-O	45.00	145.00
1844	30.00	45.00
1844-O	45.00	90.00
1845	30.00	45.00
1846	35.00	45.00
1847	30.00	45.00
1847-O	55.00	200.00
1848	50.00	175.00
1849	35.00	75.00
1849-O	800.00	2,200.00

	VG	VF
1850	35.00	135.00
1850-O	45.00	150.00
1851	65.00	200.00
1851-O	350.00	950.00
1852	60.00	185.00
1852-O	300.00	1,250.00

1853-O Seated Liberty quarter with arrows at date, reverse rays.

Arrows at Date, Reverse Rays	VG	VF
1853	30.00	45.00
1853-O	45.00	85.00

1854 Seated Liberty quarter with reverse rays removed.

Reverse Rays Removed	VG	VF
1854	30.00	40.00
1854-O	35.00	60.00
1855	30.00	40.00
1855-O	60.00	250.00
1855-S	60.00	225.00

1857-S Seated Liberty quarter with arrows at date removed.

Arrows at Date Removed	VG	VF
1859-O	35.00	65.00
1859-S	25.00	900.00
1860	35.00	50.00
1860-O	45.00	70.00
1860-S	1,000.00	3,700.00
1861	35.00	45.00
1861-S	16.00	750.00
1862	35.00	50.00
1862-S	130.00	475.00

Arrows at Date Removed	VG	VF
1863	60.00	140.00
1864	100.00	225.00
1864-S	650.00	2,150.00
1865	95.00	235.00
1865-S	180.00	400.00

1873 Seated Liberty quarter with "In God We Trust" above eagle.

"In God We Trust" Above Eagle	VG	VF
1866	600.00	1,050.00
1866-S	390.00	1,400.00
1867	325.00	850.00
1867-S	450.00	1,350.00
1868	200.00	385.00
1868-S	185.00	450.00
1869	450.00	700.00
1869-S	185.00	475.00
1870	65.00	190.00
1870-CC	14,500.00	24,500.00
1871	45.00	125.00
1871-CC	7,500.00	15,500.00
1871-S	525.00	1,150.00
1872	55.00	110.00
1872-CC	1,850.00	6,000.00
1872-S	1,250.00	3,350.00
1873, closed 3	425.00	800.00
1873, open 3	45.00	130.00
1873-CC, six known	350.00	750.00

1874 Seated Liberty quarter with arrows at date.

Arrows at Date	VG	VF
1873	30.00	60.00
1873-CC	5,750.00	16,500.00
1873-S	45.00	175.00
1874	30.00	60.00
1874-S	35.00	110.00

1886 Seated Liberty quarter.

Arrows at Date Removed	VG	VF
1875	30.00	40.00
1875-CC	155.00	450.00
1875-S	50.00	110.00
1876	30.00	40.00
1876-CC	70.00	100.00
1876-S	30.00	40.00
1877	30.00	40.00
1877-CC	70.00	100.00
1877-S	30.00	40.00
1878	30.00	40.00
1878-CC	75.00	140.00
1878-S	225.00	475.00
1879	235.00	325.00
1880	215.00	325.00
1881	250.00	350.00
1882	250.00	350.00
1883	250.00	365.00
1884	285.00	550.00
1885	225.00	285.00
1886	450.00	750.00
1887	300.00	450.00
1888	275.00	425.00
1888-S	30.00	40.00
1889	275.00	350.00
1890	75.00	135.00
1891	30.00	40.00
1891-O	325.00	750.00
1891-S	30.00	45.00

BARBER QUARTERS

The dime, quarter, and half dollar were all revised in 1892 to depict a right-facing portrait of Liberty designed by U.S. Mint Chief Engraver Charles Barber, for whom they have been popularly named.

1903 Barber quarter.

	F	XF
1892	30.00	100.00
1892-O	55.00	155.00
1892-S	135.00	300.00
1893	25.00	70.00
1893-O	45.00	165.00
1893-S	80.00	255.00
1894	35.00	95.00
1894-O	50.00	165.00
1894-S	50.00	180.00
1895	30.00	80.00
1895-O	60.00	175.00
1895-S	85.00	235.00
1896	25.00	80.00
1896-O	185.00	590.00
1896-S	2,350.00	5,250.00
1897	20.00	70.00
1897-O	185.00	420.00
1897-S	300.00	590.00
1898	25.00	75.00
1898-O	75.00	300.00
1898-S	50.00	100.00
1899	25.00	75.00
1899-O	40.00	145.00
1899-S	70.00	145.00
1900	25.00	70.00
1900-O	70.00	175.00
1900-S	40.00	80.00
1901	30.00	80.00
1901-O	200.00	590.00
1901-S	18,500.00	31,000.00
1902	20.00	65.00
1902-O	50.00	150.00
1902-S	55.00	170.00
1903	20.00	60.00

	F	XF
1903-O	40.00	125.00
1903-S	45.00	145.00
1904	20.00	70.00
1904-D	70.00	225.00
1905	35.00	70.00
1905-O	115.00	265.00
1905-S	60.00	110.00
1906	18.50	35.00
1906-D	25.00	70.00
1906-O	40.00	110.00
1907	17.00	60.00
1907-D	30.00	75.00
1907-O	20.00	65.00
1907-S	50.00	135.00
1908	18.50	65.00
1908-D	17.50	65.00
1908-O	17.50	70.00
1908-S	90.00	300.00
1909	17.50	65.00
1909-D	20.00	85.00
1909-O	300.00	625.00
1909-S	35.00	90.00
1910	30.00	80.00
1910-D	45.00	130.00
1911	20.00	70.00
1911-D	145.00	450.00
1911-S	50.00	210.00
1912	17.50	55.00
1912-S	45.00	130.00
1913	75.00	390.00
1913-D	40.00	90.00
1913-S	5,250.00	10,500.00
1914	17.00	55.00
1914-D	17.00	55.00
1914-S	400.00	885.00
1915	17.00	60.00
1915-D	17.00	60.00
1915-S	50.00	110.00
1916	17.00	55.00
1916-D	17.00	55.00

STANDING LIBERTY QUARTERS

The Standing Liberty design, by Hermon A. MacNeil, is considered one of the most beautiful in U.S. coinage history. The design originally depicted Liberty with her right breast exposed (Type 1). Because of public backlash, the design was modified so Liberty's breast was covered (Type 2).

The design was further modified in 1925. Previously, the date was in higher relief, which caused the numerals to wear off easily. In 1925, the date area was carved out, which allowed the numerals to be recessed into the design and better protect them from wear.

Liberty's head did not always strike up fully. As a result, examples with a "full head" command a premium.

1916 Standing Liberty quarter, Type 1.

Type 1	F	XF
1916	6,900.00	10,000.00
1917	65.00	120.00
1917-D	100.00	200.00
1917-S	110.00	220.00

1927 Standing Liberty quarter, Type 2.

Type 2	F	XF
1917	50.00	95.00
1917-D	90.00	160.00
1917-S	65.00	110.00
1918	30.00	45.00
1918-D	65.00	120.00
1918-S	30.00	50.00
1919	55.00	80.00

Type 2	F	XF
1919-D	200.00	565.00
1919-S	185.00	510.00
1920	25.00	50.00
1920-D	90.00	160.00
1920-S	30.00	55.00
1921	450.00	825.00
1923	35.00	55.00
1923-S	675.00	1,500.00
1924	25.00	45.00
1924-D	110.00	185.00
1924-S	45.00	100.00
1925	9.50	45.00
1926	8.75	30.00
1926-D	20.00	75.00
1926-S	11.00	110.00
1927	8.75	40.00
1927-D	30.00	140.00
1927-S	110.00	1,000.00
1928	8.75	30.00
1928-D	9.50	45.00
1929	8.75	30.00
1929-D	9.50	40.00
1929-S	9.25	35.00
1930	8.75	30.00
1930-S	8.75	35.00

WASHINGTON QUARTERS

The Washington quarter was intended to be a one-year issue commemorating the 200th anniversary of George Washington's birth, but it proved to be so popular that it permanently replaced the Standing Liberty quarter. John Flanagan's design is based on a 1785 bust of Washington by sculptor Jean Antoine Houdon.

	VF	MS-60
1932	7.00	25.00
1932-D	180.00	1,150.00
1932-S	165.00	465.00
1934	7.50	25.00
1934-D	20.00	250.00

1936-D Washington quarter.

	VF	MS-60
1935	7.50	20.00
1935-D	16.50	245.00
1935-S	9.00	95.00
1936	7.50	25.00
1936-D	25.00	585.00
1936-S	8.50	110.00
1937	9.00	20.00
1937-D	8.25	70.00
1937-S	20.00	160.00
1938	8.25	90.00
1938-S	9.75	110.00
1939	7.50	15.00
1939-D	9.00	40.00
1939-S	12.00	100.00
1940	7.50	17.50
1940-D	12.50	130.00
1940-S	7.00	30.00
1941	6.00	9.50
1941-D	7.00	35.00
1941-S	7.50	30.00
1942	6.00	8.25
1942-D	7.00	18.00
1942-S	7.25	70.00
1943	6.00	8.25
1943-D	7.50	30.00
1943-S	7.50	25.00
1944	6.00	7.50
1944-D	7.00	20.00
1944-S	7.00	15.00
1945	6.00	7.50

	VF	MS-60
1945-D	7.00	18.00
1945-S	7.00	8.50
1946	6.00	7.25
1946-D	7.00	9.75
1946-S	7.00	8.25
1947	7.00	11.50
1947-D	7.00	11.00
1947-S	7.00	9.25
1948	7.00	8.50
1948-D	7.00	13.00
1948-S	7.00	8.50
1949	7.00	35.00
1949-D	7.00	16.50
1950	7.00	10.00
1950-D	6.00	7.50
1950-S	7.00	13.50
1951	6.00	8.00
1951-D	6.00	9.00
1951-S	7.00	20.00
1952	6.00	10.50
1952-D	6.00	8.50
1952-S	7.00	15.00
1953	7.00	10.00
1953-D	6.00	8.00
1953-S	6.00	8.00
1954	6.00	7.25
1954-D	6.00	7.25
1954-S	6.00	8.00
1955	6.00	7.25
1955-D	7.00	8.25
1956	6.00	7.25
1956-D	6.00	7.25
1957	6.00	7.25
1957-D	6.00	7.25
1958	6.00	7.25
1958-D	6.00	7.25
1959	6.00	7.25
1959-D	6.00	7.25
1960	6.00	7.25
1960-D	6.00	7.25
1961	6.00	7.25

	VF	MS-60
1961-D	6.00	7.25
1962	6.00	7.25
1962-D	6.00	7.25
1963	6.00	7.25
1963-D	6.00	7.25
1964	6.00	7.25
1964-D	6.00	7.25

Clad Composition	VF	MS-60
1965	12.00	—
1966	7.50	—
1967	12.00	—
1968	15.00	—
1968-D	8.00	—
1968-S	—	2.00
1969	14.00	—
1969-D	10.00	—
1969-S	—	2.25
1970	12.00	—
1970-D	6.00	—
1970-S	—	2.00
1971	15.00	—
1971-D	6.50	—
1971-S	—	2.00
1972	7.50	—
1972-D	10.00	—
1972-S	—	2.00
1973	10.00	—
1973-D	11.00	—
1973-S	—	1.75
1974	8.00	—
1974-D	15.00	—
1974-S	—	2.00

BICENTENNIAL REVERSE

A variety of coinage proposals for the nation's bicentennial emerged in the years leading up to the celebration. Among them were proposals for special commemorative coins (the U.S. Mint had not issued commemorative coins since 1954), redesigning all six circulating coins, issuing a two-cent coin with a Bicentennial design, and issuing a gold commemorative coin. The Mint and Treasury Department initially resisted any changes to circulating coin designs and the issuance of commemorative coins, but they eased their opposition as the various proposals were winnowed to a final bill that was signed into law Oct. 18, 1973, by President Richard M. Nixon. That bill called for quarters, half dollars, and dollar coins struck after July 4, 1975, to bear new reverse designs emblematic of the nation's Bicentennial. The law also called for the coins to bear the dual date "1776-1976."

The law also authorized the Mint to strike the Bicentennial coins in a 40-percent silver composition for inclusion in three-coin uncirculated and proof sets for sale directly to collectors.

To select designs for the Bicentennial coins, the Mint sponsored a contest open to all U.S. citizens. Jack L. Ahr of Arlington Heights, Ill., had his Revolutionary-era drummer-boy design selected for the quarter.

1976 Washington Bicentennial quarter.

Bicentennial Reverse	MS-65	PF-65
1976	8.00	—
1976-D	10.00	—
1976-S	—	3.25
1976-S silver	6.00	4.50

REGULAR REVERSE RESUMED

Starting in 1992, Washington quarters in the traditional 90-percent silver composition were struck for inclusion in silver proof sets, which also included silver dimes and silver half dollars.

Regular Reverse Resumed	MS-65	PF-65
1977	10.00	—
1977-D	8.00	—
1977-S	—	2.75
1978	9.00	—
1978-D	11.00	—
1978-S	—	2.75
1979	10.00	—
1979-D	9.00	—
1979-S	—	2.50
1980-P	8.00	—
1980-D	8.50	—
1980-S	—	2.75
1981-P	8.00	—
1981-D	6.50	—
1981-S	—	2.75
1982-P	28.00	—
1982-D	15.00	—
1982-S	—	2.75
1983-P	45.00	—
1983-D	30.00	—
1983-S	—	3.00
1984-P	14.50	—
1984-D	12.50	—
1984-S	—	2.75
1985-P	12.50	—
1985-D	10.00	—
1985-S	—	2.75
1986-P	12.00	—
1986-D	15.00	—
1986-S	—	3.00
1987-P	10.00	—
1987-D	10.00	—
1987-S	—	2.75
1988-P	16.00	—
1988-D	14.00	—
1988-S	—	2.75
1989-P	18.00	—
1989-D	7.50	—
1989-S	—	2.75
1990-P	17.00	—
1990-D	7.00	—

Regular Reverse Resumed	MS-65	PF-65
1990-S	—	4.50
1991-P	15.00	—
1991-D	12.00	—
1991-S	—	2.75
1992-P	20.00	—
1992-D	27.50	—
1992-S	—	2.75
1992-S silver	—	7.00
1993-P	11.00	—
1993-D	14.00	—
1993-S	—	2.75
1993-S silver	—	7.00
1994-P	18.00	—
1994-D	10.00	—
1994-S	—	2.75
1994-S silver	—	8.00
1995-P	12.00	—
1995-D	10.00	—
1995-S	—	8.50
1995-S silver	—	8.00
1996-P	12.00	—
1996-D	14.00	—
1996-S	—	4.50
1996-S silver	—	8.00
1997-P	12.50	—
1997-D	16.00	—
1997-S	—	8.50
1997-S silver	—	8.00
1998-P	13.50	—
1998-D	13.50	—
1998-S	—	8.50
1998-S silver	—	7.00

50 STATE QUARTERS

President Bill Clinton signed the 50 States Commemorative Coin Act into law on Dec. 1, 1997. The bill provided that from 1999 through 2008, the quarter's reverse would be redesigned to honor each of the 50 states. Five new designs would be introduced each year, and each new design would honor a different state. The states would be honored in the order in which they ratified the Constitution or were admitted to the union.

The bill gave authority for final approval of the designs to the Treasury secretary. It required the secretary to consult with each state's governor or the governor's designee on the respective state's design. The law banned any "frivolous or inappropriate" design. It further prohibited the depiction of a head-and-shoulders bust of any person, living or dead, or any representation of a living person. The traditional bust of George Washington appears on the obverse of each coin.

The law also authorized the U.S. Mint to produce uncirculated and proof examples of the 50 State Quarters for sale to collectors and to produce examples in 90-percent silver composition for sale to collectors.

Delaware	MS-65	PF-65
1999-P	5.00	—
1999-D	7.00	—
1999-S	—	3.50
1999-S silver	—	20.00

Pennsylvania	MS-65	PF-65
1999-P	5.00	—
1999-D	4.00	—
1999-S	—	3.50
1999-S silver	—	20.00

New Jersey	MS-65	PF-65
1999-P	5.00	—
1999-D	4.00	—
1999-S	—	3.50
1999-S silver	—	20.00

Georgia	MS-65	PF-65
1999-P	4.50	—
1999-D	4.50	—
1999-S	—	3.50
1999-S silver	—	20.00

Connecticut	MS-65	PF-65
1999-P	6.00	—
1999-D	5.00	—
1999-S	—	3.50
1999-S silver	—	20.00

Massachusetts	MS-65	PF-65
2000-P	7.00	—
2000-D	8.00	—
2000-S	—	3.00
2000-S silver	—	9.00

Maryland	MS-65	PF-65
2000-P	6.00	—
2000-D	6.00	—
2000-S	—	3.00
2000-S silver	—	9.00

South Carolina	MS-65	PF-65
2000-P	6.00	—
2000-D	9.00	—
2000-S	—	3.00
2000-S silver	—	9.00

New Hampshire	MS-65	PF-65
2000-P	8.00	—
2000-D	9.00	—
2000-S	—	3.00
2000-S silver	—	9.00

Virginia	MS-65	PF-65
2000-P	6.50	—
2000-D	6.50	—
2000-S	—	3.00
2000-S silver	—	9.50

New York	MS-65	PF-65
2001-P	5.50	—
2001-D	5.50	—
2001-S	—	4.00
2001-S silver	—	9.50

North Carolina	MS-65	PF-65
2001-P	5.50	—
2001-D	6.50	—
2001-S	—	4.00
2001-S silver	—	9.50

Rhode Island	MS-65	PF-65
2001-P	5.50	—
2001-D	6.00	—
2001-S	—	4.00
2001-S silver	—	9.50

Vermont	MS-65	PF-65
2001-P	6.50	—
2001-D	6.50	—
2001-S	—	4.00
2001-S silver	—	9.50

Kentucky	MS-65	PF-65
2001-P	6.50	—
2001-D	7.00	—
2001-S	—	4.00
2001-S silver	—	9.50

Tennessee	MS-65	PF-65
2002-P	6.50	—
2002-D	7.00	—
2002-S	—	2.50
2002-S silver	—	8.50

Ohio	MS-65	PF-65
2002-P	5.50	—
2002-D	5.50	—
2002-S	—	2.50
2002-S silver	—	8.50

Louisiana	MS-65	PF-65
2002-P	5.50	—
2002-D	6.00	—
2002-S	—	2.50
2002-S silver	—	8.50

Indiana	MS-65	PF-65
2002-P	5.00	—
2002-D	5.00	—
2002-S	—	2.50
2002-S silver	—	8.50

Mississippi	MS-65	PF-65
2002-P	5.00	—
2002-D	5.00	—
2002-S	—	2.50
2002-S silver	—	8.50

Illinois	MS-65	PF-65
2003-P	5.00	—
2003-D	5.00	—
2003-S	—	2.50
2003-S silver	—	8.50

Alabama	MS-65	PF-65
2003-P	5.00	—
2003-D	5.00	—
2003-S	—	2.50
2003-S silver	—	8.50

Maine	MS-65	PF-65
2003-P	5.00	—
2003-D	5.00	—
2003-S	—	2.50
2003-S silver	—	8.50

Missouri	MS-65	PF-65
2003-P	5.00	—
2003-D	5.00	—
2003-S	—	2.50
2003-S silver	—	8.50

Arkansas	MS-65	PF-65
2003-P	5.00	—
2003-D	5.00	—
2003-S	—	2.50
2003-S silver	—	8.50

Michigan	MS-65	PF-65
2004-P	5.00	—
2004-D	5.00	—
2004-S	—	2.50
2004-S silver	—	8.50

Florida	MS-65	PF-65
2004-P	5.00	—
2004-D	5.00	—
2004-S	—	2.50
2004-S silver	—	8.50

Texas	MS-65	PF-65
2004-P	5.00	—
2004-D	5.00	—
2004-S	—	2.50
2004-S silver	—	8.50

Iowa	MS-65	PF-65
2004-P	5.00	—
2004-D	5.00	—
2004-S	—	2.50
2004-S silver	—	8.50

Wisconsin	MS-65	PF-65
2004-P	5.00	—
2004-D	5.00	—
2004-S	—	2.50
2004-S silver	—	8.50

Minnesota	MS-65	PF-65
2005-P	5.00	—
2005-P satin finish	4.50	—
2005-D	5.00	—
2005-D satin finish	4.50	—
2005-S	—	2.50
2005-S silver	—	8.50

Oregon	MS-65	PF-65
2005-P	5.00	—
2005-P satin finish	4.50	—
2005-D	5.00	—
2005-D satin finish	4.50	—
2005-S	—	2.50
2005-S silver	—	8.50

Kansas	MS-65	PF-65
2005-P	5.00	—
2005-P satin finish	4.50	—
2005-D	5.00	—
2005-D satin finish	4.50	—
2005-S	—	2.50
2005-S silver	—	8.50

West Virginia	MS-65	PF-65
2005-P	5.00	—
2005-P satin finish	4.50	—
2005-D	5.00	—
2005-D satin finish	4.50	—
2005-S	—	2.50
2005-S silver	—	8.50

California	MS-65	PF-65
2005-P	5.00	—
2005-P satin finish	4.50	—
2005-D	5.00	—
2005-D satin finish	4.50	—
2005-S	—	2.50
2005-S silver	—	8.50

Nevada	MS-65	PF-65
2006-P	5.00	—
2006-P satin finish	4.50	—
2006-D	5.00	—
2006-D satin finish	4.50	—
2006-S	—	2.50
2006-S silver	—	8.50

Nebraska	MS-65	PF-65
2006-P	5.00	—
2006-P satin finish	4.50	—
2006-D	5.00	—
2006-D satin finish	4.50	—
2006-S	—	2.50
2006-S silver	—	8.50

Colorado	MS-65	PF-65
2006-P	5.00	—
2006-P satin finish	4.50	—
2006-D	5.00	—
2006-D satin finish	4.50	—
2006-S	—	2.50
2006-S silver	—	8.50

North Dakota	MS-65	PF-65
2006-P	5.00	—
2006-P satin finish	4.50	—
2006-D	5.00	—v
2006-D satin finish	4.50	—
2006-S	—	2.50
2006-S silver	—	8.50

South Dakota	MS-65	PF-65
2006-P	5.00	—
2006-P satin finish	4.50	—
2006-D	5.00	—
2006-D satin finish	4.50	—
2006-S	—	2.50
2006-S silver	—	8.50

Montana	MS-65	PF-65
2007-P	5.00	—
2007-P satin finish	4.50	—
2007-D	5.00	—
2007-D satin finish	4.50	—
2007-S	—	2.50
2007-S silver	—	8.50

Washington	MS-65	PF-65
2007-P	5.00	—
2007-P satin finish	4.50	—
2007-D	5.00	—
2007-D satin finish	4.50	—
2007-S	—	2.50
2007-S silver	—	8.50

Idaho	MS-65	PF-65
2007-P	5.00	—
2007-P satin finish	4.50	—
2007-D	5.00	—
2007-D satin finish	4.50	—
2007-S	—	2.50
2007-S silver	—	8.50

Wyoming	MS-65	PF-65
2007-P	5.00	—
2007-P satin finish	4.50	—
2007-D	5.00	—
2007-D satin finish	4.50	—
2007-S	—	2.50
2007-S silver	—	8.50

Utah	MS-65	PF-65
2007-P	5.00	—
2007-P satin finish	4.50	—
2007-D	5.00	—
2007-D satin finish	4.50	—
2007-S	—	2.50
2007-S silver	—	8.50

Oklahoma	MS-65	PF-65
2008-P	5.00	—
2008-P satin finish	4.50	—
2008-D	5.00	—
2008-D satin finish	4.50	—
2008-S	—	2.50
2008-S silver	—	8.50

New Mexico	MS-65	PF-65
2008-P	5.00	—
2008-P satin finish	4.50	—
2008-D	5.00	—
2008-D satin finish	4.50	—
2008-S	—	2.50
2008-S silver	—	8.50

Arizona	MS-65	PF-65
2008-P	5.00	—
2008-P satin finish	4.50	—
2008-D	5.00	—
2008-D satin finish	4.50	—
2008-S	—	2.50
2008-S silver	—	8.50

Alaska	MS-65	PF-65
2008-P	5.00	—
2008-P satin finish	4.50	—
2008-D	5.00	—
2008-D satin finish	4.50	—
2008-S	—	2.50
2008-S silver	—	8.50

Hawaii	MS-65	PF-65
2008-P	5.00	—
2008-P satin finish	4.50	—
2008-D	5.00	—
2008-D satin finish	4.50	—
2008-S	—	2.50
2008-S silver	—	8.50

DISTRICT OF COLUMBIA AND U.S. TERRITORIES QUARTERS

Upon completion of the 50 State Quarters program, the U.S. Mint issued circulating quarters honoring the District of Columbia and the five U.S. territories in 2009. The coins were released in two-month intervals beginning with the District of Columbia quarter in February 2009. It was followed, in order, by coins honoring Puerto Rico, Guam, American Samoa, U.S. Virgin Islands, and the Northern Mariana Islands.

The traditional bust of George Washington appears on the obverse of each coin. As with the State Quarters, the authorizing legislation provided for uncirculated, proof, and 90-percent silver versions of the coins for sale to collectors.

District of Columbia	MS-65	PF-65
2009-P	5.00	—
2009-D	5.00	—
2009-S	—	3.75
2009-S silver	—	7.75

Puerto Rico	MS-65	PF-65
2009-P	5.00	—
2009-D	5.00	—
2009-S	—	3.75
2009-S silver	—	7.75

Guam	MS-65	PF-65
2009-P	5.00	—
2009-D	5.00	—
2009-S	—	3.75
2009-S silver	—	7.75

American Samoa	MS-65	PF-65
2009-P	5.00	—
2009-D	5.00	—
2009-S	—	3.75
2009-S silver	—	7.75

U.S. Virgin Islands	MS-65	PF-65
2009-P	5.00	—
2009-D	5.00	—
2009-S	—	3.75
2009-S silver	—	7.75

Northern Mariana Island	MS-65	PF-65
2009-P	5.00	—
2009-D	5.00	—
2009-S	—	3.75
2009-S silver	—	7.75

AMERICA THE BEAUTIFUL QUARTERS

The America the Beautiful Quarters program (a U.S. Mint trademark) will continue the issuance of circulating quarters with commemorative reverse designs. Five different reverse designs honoring national parks and national sites will be issued in each year from 2010 through 2020. The final issue in the 56-coin series is scheduled for release in 2021. Every state, every U.S. territory, and the District of Columbia will be represented in the series. The traditional bust of George Washington will appear on the obverse of each coin.

Like the state and territories quarters, the authorizing legislation again provides for the issuance of uncirculated, proof, and 90-percent silver versions of the coins for sale to collectors.

Hot Springs	MS-65	PF-65
2010-P	5.00	—
2010-D	5.00	—
2010-S	—	3.75
2010-S silver	—	7.75

Yellowstone	MS-65	PF-65
2010-P	5.00	—
2010-D	5.00	—
2010-S	—	3.75
2010-S silver	—	7.75

Yosemite	MS-65	PF-65
2010-P	5.00	—
2010-D	5.00	—
2010-S	—	3.75
2010-S silver	—	7.75

Grand Canyon	MS-65	PF-65
2010-P	5.00	—
2010-D	5.00	—
2010-S	—	3.75
2010-S silver	—	7.75

Mount Hood	MS-65	PF-65
2010-P	5.00	—
2010-D	5.00	—
2010-S	—	3.75
2010-S silver	—	7.75

Gettysburg	MS-65	PF-65
2011-P	5.00	—
2011-D	5.00	—
2011-S	—	3.75
2011-S silver	—	7.75

Glacier	MS-65	PF-65
2011-P	5.00	—
2011-D	5.00	—
2011-S	—	3.75
2011-S silver	—	7.75

Olympic	MS-65	PF-65
2011-P	5.00	—
2011-D	5.00	—
2011-S	—	3.75
2011-S silver	—	7.75

Vicksburg	MS-65	PF-65
2011-P	5.00	—
2011-D	5.00	—
2011-S	—	3.75
2011-S silver	—	7.75

Chickasaw	MS-65	PF-65
2011-P	5.00	—
2011-D	5.00	—
2011-S	—	3.75
2011-S silver	—	7.75

El Yunque	MS-65	PF-65
2012-P	5.00	—
2012-D	5.00	—
2012-S	—	3.75
2012-S silver	—	7.75

Chaco Culture	MS-65	PF-65
2012-P	8.00	—
2012-D	8.00	—
2012-S	—	4.00
2012-S silver	—	7.75

Acadia	MS-65	PF-65
2012-P	5.00	—
2012-D	5.00	—
2012-S	—	3.75
2012-S silver	—	7.75

Hawai'i Volcanoes	MS-65	PF-65
2012-P	5.00	—
2012-D	5.00	—
2012-S	—	3.75
2012-S silver	—	7.75

Denali	MS-65	PF-65
2012-P	5.00	—
2012-D	5.00	—
2012-S	—	3.75
2012-S silver	—	7.75

2013

White Mountain National Forest, New Hampshire

Perry's Victory and International Peace Memorial, Ohio

Great Basin National Park, Nevada

Fort McHenry National Monument and Historic Shrine, Maryland

Mount Rushmore National Memorial, South Dakota

2014

Great Smoky Mountains National Park, Tennessee

Shenandoah National Park, Virginia

Arches National Park, Utah

Great Sand Dunes National Park, Colorado

Everglades National Park, Florida

2015

Homestead National Monument of America, Nebraska

Kisatchie National Forest, Louisiana

Blue Ridge Parkway, North Carolina

Bombay Hook National Wildlife Refuge, Delaware

Saratoga National Historic Park, New York

2016

Shawnee National Forest, Illinois

Cumberland Gap National Historical Park, Kentucky

Harpers Ferry National Historical Park, West Virginia

Theodore Roosevelt National Park, North Dakota

Fort Moultrie (Fort Sumter National Monument), South Carolina

2017

Effigy Mounds National Monument, Iowa

Frederick Douglass National Historic Site, District of Columbia

Ozark National Scenic Riverways, Missouri

Ellis Island National Monument (Statue of Liberty), New Jersey

George Rogers Clark National Historical Park, Indiana

2018

Pictured Rocks National Lakeshore, Michigan

Apostle Islands National Lakeshore, Wisconsin

Voyageurs National Park, Minnesota

Cumberland Island National Seashore, Georgia

Block Island National Wildlife Refuge, Rhode Island

2019

Lowell National Historical Park, Massachusetts

American Memorial Park, Northern Mariana Islands

War in the Pacific National Historical Park, Guam

San Antonio Missions National Historical Park, Texas

Frank Church-River of No Return Wilderness, Idaho

2020

National Park of American Samoa

Weir Farm National Historic Site, Connecticut

Salt River Bay National Historical Park and Ecological Preserve, U.S. Virgin Islands

Marsh-Billings-Rockefeller National Historical Park, Vermont

Tallgrass Prairie National Preserve, Kansas

2021

Tuskegee Airmen National Historic Site, Alabama

SEATED LIBERTY HALF DOLLARS

Christian Gobrecht's Seated Liberty design first appeared on the dollar and was later adapted for the lower denominations. The Seated Liberty half dollar underwent a number of modifications in design and specifications during its long run. In some cases, a design tweak indicated a change in specifications. In 1839, drapery was added to Liberty's left elbow.

1842 Seated Liberty half dollar.

	VG	VF
1839 no drapery	90.00	900.00
1839 with drapery	45.00	185.00
1840	45.00	100.00
1840-O	45.00	100.00
1841	65.00	165.00
1841-O	65.00	100.00
1842	40.00	140.00
1842-O	45.00	175.00
1843	40.00	135.00
1843-O	50.00	165.00
1844	45.00	160.00
1844-O	45.00	165.00
1845	45.00	220.00
1845-O no drapery	70.00	350.00
1845-O with drapery	45.00	165.00
1846	45.00	175.00
1846-O	45.00	220.00
1847	45.00	130.00
1847-O	45.00	145.00
1848	75.00	275.00
1848-O	45.00	175.00
1849	45.00	135.00
1849-O	45.00	175.00
1850	325.00	700.00
1850-O	45.00	175.00
1851	475.00	1,350.00
1851-O	55.00	225.00
1852	500.00	1,100.00
1852-O	125.00	750.00
1853-O rare	7.00	15.00

1853 Seated Liberty half dollar with arrows at date, reverse rays.

Arrows at Date, Reverse Rays	VG	VF
1853	40.00	90.00
1853-O	50.00	115.00

1854 Seated Liberty half dollar with reverse rays removed.

Reverse Rays Removed	VG	VF
1854	40.00	70.00
1854-O	40.00	70.00
1855	40.00	80.00
1855-O	45.00	70.00
1855-S	575.00	1,600.00
1856	40.00	70.00
1856-O	40.00	70.00
1856-S	110.00	275.00
1857	40.00	70.00
1857-O	45.00	85.00
1857-S	125.00	375.00
1858	40.00	70.00
1858-O	40.00	70.00
1858-S	65.00	140.00
1859	45.00	90.00
1859-O	40.00	70.00
1859-S	45.00	100.00
1860	45.00	100.00
1860-O	40.00	70.00
1860-S	45.00	80.00
1861	45.00	70.00
1861-O	45.00	80.00
1861-S	50.00	85.00
1862	65.00	120.00
1862-S	45.00	70.00
1863	60.00	110.00
1863-S	55.00	90.00
1864	75.00	150.00
1864-S	55.00	125.00
1865	60.00	100.00
1865-S	50.00	100.00
1866 proof, one known	—	—
1866-S	650.00	1,250.00

Motto Above Eagle	VG	VF
1866	55.00	95.00
1866-S	50.00	85.00
1867	55.00	130.00
1867-S	50.00	70.00
1868	70.00	185.00
1868-S	40.00	70.00
1869	55.00	85.00
1869-S	55.00	95.00
1870	45.00	80.00
1870-CC	1,850.00	7,250.00
1870-S	45.00	95.00
1871	40.00	75.00
1871-CC	400.00	1,275.00
1871-S	40.00	70.00
1872	50.00	75.00
1872-CC	175.00	750.00
1872-S	50.00	135.00
1873 closed 3	45.00	115.00
1873 open 3	4,450.00	6,600.00
1873-CC	325.00	950.00

1873 Seated Liberty half dollar with arrows at date.

Arrows at Date	VG	VF
1873	55.00	120.00
1873-CC	400.00	1,100.00
1873-S	110.00	245.00
1874	40.00	85.00
1874-CC	1,000.00	3,250.00
1874-S	65.00	185.00
Arrows at Date Removed	**VG**	**VF**
1875	35.00	65.00
1875-CC	80.00	225.00
1875-S	35.00	75.00
1876	35.00	65.00
1876-CC	60.00	115.00
1876-S	35.00	65.00

1878-S Seated Liberty half dollar with arrows removed from date.

Arrows at Date Removed	VG	VF
1877	35.00	65.00
1877-CC	70.00	125.00
1877-S	35.00	65.00
1878	45.00	90.00
1878-CC	1,150.00	2,350.00
1878-S	42,000.00	58,000.00
1879	310.00	450.00
1880	300.00	410.00
1881	325.00	400.00
1882	410.00	600.00
1883	390.00	560.00
1884	425.00	610.00
1885	450.00	575.00
1886	550.00	725.00
1887	600.00	800.00
1888	310.00	410.00
1889	315.00	465.00
1890	310.00	415.00
1891	75.00	125.00

BARBER HALF DOLLARS

The dime, quarter, and half dollar were all revised in 1892 to depict a right-facing portrait of Liberty designed by U.S. Mint Chief Engraver Charles Barber, for whom they have been popularly named.

Barber half dollars are common, and well-worn examples are worth bullion value only. But the series is popular among collectors, resulting in solid demand and, thus, strong values in middle grades.

	VG	VF
1892	40.00	120.00
1892-O	420.00	575.00
1892-S	330.00	530.00

1892 Barber half dollar.

	VG	VF
1893	35.00	135.00
1893-O	65.00	220.00
1893-S	225.00	500.00
1894	50.00	200.00
1894-O	35.00	170.00
1894-S	30.00	125.00
1895	25.00	150.00
1895-O	45.00	195.00
1895-S	55.00	235.00
1896	30.00	160.00
1896-O	55.00	290.00
1896-S	145.00	350.00
1897	20.00	100.00
1897-O	230.00	835.00
1897-S	225.00	535.00
1898	20.00	95.00
1898-O	75.00	355.00
1898-S	55.00	175.00
1899	20.00	100.00
1899-O	40.00	170.00
1899-S	45.00	135.00
1900	20.00	90.00
1900-O	25.00	165.00
1900-S	20.00	100.00
1901	20.00	95.00
1901-O	25.00	200.00
1901-S	55.00	355.00
1902	15.00	85.00
1902-O	17.00	100.00

	VG	VF
1902-S	20.00	150.00
1903	20.00	100.00
1903-O	17.00	115.00
1903-S	20.00	125.00
1904	15.00	85.00
1904-O	30.00	220.00
1904-S	75.00	555.00
1905	35.00	180.00
1905-O	45.00	235.00
1905-S	20.00	125.00
1906	15.00	85.00
1906-D	15.00	90.00
1906-O	15.00	100.00
1906-S	17.00	110.00
1907	15.00	85.00
1907-D	15.00	75.00
1907-O	15.00	90.00
1907-S	20.00	165.00
1908	15.00	80.00
1908-D	15.00	80.00
1908-O	15.00	90.00
1908-S	25.00	160.00
1909	20.00	85.00
1909-O	25.00	140.00
1909-S	15.00	100.00
1910	30.00	170.00
1910-S	20.00	100.00
1911	15.00	85.00
1911-D	20.00	90.00
1911-S	20.00	100.00
1912	15.00	85.00
1912-D	15.00	80.00
1912-S	20.00	100.00
1913	90.00	420.00
1913-D	20.00	100.00
1913-S	25.00	110.00
1914	175.00	550.00
1914-S	20.00	100.00
1915	170.00	380.00
1915-D	15.00	75.00
1915-S	20.00	95.00

WALKING LIBERTY HALF DOLLARS

Adolph Weinman's Walking Liberty half-dollar design is an all-time favorite among collectors. (Weinman also designed the Mercury dime.) The design was reprised in 1986 for the new silver American Eagle bullion coins.

Mint marks on the Walking Liberty half dollar originally appeared on the obverse, but they were moved to the reverse in 1917. Watch for genuine 1916 and 1938 examples with mint marks fraudulently added to emulate the more rare 1916-S and 1938-D.

Liberty's head did not always strike up fully. High-grade examples with Liberty's head fully struck command a premium.

1921 Walking Liberty half dollar.

	F	XF
1916	95.00	240.00
1916-D	80.00	220.00
1916-S	280.00	600.00
1917 reverse mint mark	15.00	40.00
1917-D obverse mint mark	80.00	235.00
1917-S obverse mint mark	135.00	700.00
1917-D reverse mint mark	45.00	275.00
1917-S reverse mint mark	17.00	65.00
1918	15.00	150.00
1918-D	35.00	225.00
1918-S	16.00	60.00
1919	80.00	535.00
1919-D	95.00	765.00
1919-S	70.00	825.00
1920	15.00	75.00

	F	XF
1920-D	65.00	460.00
1920-S	20.00	235.00
1921	350.00	1,575.00
1921-D	550.00	2,200.00
1921-S	210.00	4,850.00
1923-S	30.00	300.00
1927-S	17.00	165.00
1928-S	20.00	200.00
1929-D	18.00	100.00
1929-S	15.00	115.00
1933-S	18.00	60.00
1934	15.00	17.00
1934-D	20.00	35.00
1934-S	15.00	30.00
1935	15.00	18.00
1935-D	15.00	35.00
1935-S	15.00	30.00
1936	15.00	18.00
1936-D	15.00	20.00
1936-S	15.00	20.00
1937	15.00	18.00
1937-D	17.00	35.00
1937-S	15.00	25.00
1938	15.00	20.00
1938-D	100.00	185.00
1939	15.00	18.00
1939-D	15.00	18.00
1939-S	15.00	25.00
1940	15.00	17.00
1940-S	15.00	18.00
1941	15.00	16.00
1941-D	15.00	16.00
1941-S	15.00	20.00
1942	15.00	16.00
1942-D	15.00	16.00
1942-S	15.00	16.00
1943	15.00	16.00
1943-D	15.00	16.00
1943-S	15.00	16.00
1944	15.00	16.00
1944-D	15.00	16.00

	F	XF
1944-S	15.00	16.00
1945	15.00	16.00
1945-D	15.00	16.00
1945-S	15.00	16.00
1946	15.00	16.00
1946-D	15.00	25.00
1946-S	15.00	17.00
1947	15.00	16.00
1947-D	15.00	16.00

FRANKLIN HALF DOLLARS

U.S. Mint Director Nellie Tayloe Ross was apparently the driving force behind the change from the Walking Liberty half dollar to the Franklin half dollar in 1948. Ross had wanted to introduce a coin honoring Franklin for some time. According to some historical accounts, she also considered the cent because of Franklin's saying "A penny saved is twopence clear," which evolved into "A penny saved is a penny earned."

U.S. Mint Chief Engraver John Sinnock's bust of Franklin on the obverse is a composite based on several portraits. The Liberty Bell depiction on the reverse is based on the 1926 U.S. Sesquicentennial commemorative half dollar, also designed by Sinnock. A small eagle was added to the right of the bell because coinage laws require that all denominations larger than a dime include a depiction of an eagle.

Mint-state examples with fully struck lines across the bell command a premium.

	XF	MS-60
1948	15.00	17.00
1948-D	14.50	16.00
1949	15.00	40.00
1949-D	16.50	45.00
1949-S	16.50	60.00
1950	14.00	25.00

1962 Franklin half dollar.

	XF	MS-60
1950-D	15.00	20.00
1951	13.50	17.00
1951-D	18.00	25.00
1951-S	14.50	25.00
1952	14.00	17.00
1952-D	14.00	17.00
1952-S	15.00	50.00
1953	14.50	25.00
1953-D	13.50	14.00
1953-S	14.50	25.00
1954	13.50	15.00
1954-D	13.50	15.00
1954-S	14.00	15.00
1955	18.00	20.00
1956	14.00	15.00
1957	14.00	15.00
1957-D	14.00	15.00
1958	14.00	15.00
1958-D	14.00	15.00
1959	14.00	15.00
1959-D	14.00	15.00
1960	14.00	15.00
1960-D	14.00	15.00
1961	14.00	15.00
1961-D	14.00	15.00
1962	14.00	15.00
1962-D	14.00	15.00
1963	14.00	15.00
1963-D	14.00	15.00

KENNEDY HALF DOLLARS

It was only days after John F. Kennedy's assassination on Nov. 22, 1963, when proposals to honor the slain president on a coin emerged. The quarter, half dollar, and dollar were all considered before the half dollar was chosen. Congress approved the design change quickly so production could begin with the new year's coinage in January 1964.

Work on the Kennedy half dollar began at the U.S. Mint even before the authorizing legislation was signed into law. To accommodate the tight turnaround from concept to production, it was decided to adapt artwork already in-house. Kennedy's portrait on the obverse and the presidential seal on the reverse were both based on his official presidential medal. U.S. Mint Chief Engraver Gilroy Roberts had designed the medal's obverse, so he worked on adapting it for the half dollar. His assistant engraver, Frank Gasparro, who later succeeded Roberts as chief engraver, had designed the medal's reverse, so he worked on adapting it for the half dollar.

Kennedy half dollars have been struck in several different compositions, as noted in the listings that follow.

Coins dated 1970-D, 1987-P, and 1987-D were not issued for circulation but are widely available from broken-up Mint uncirculated sets.

1964 Kennedy half dollar.

90-Percent Silver Composition	MS-65	PF-65
1964	20.00	15.00
1964-D	24.00	—

40-Percent Silver Composition	MS-65	PF-65
1965	14.50	—
1966	22.00	—
1967	18.50	—
1968-D	16.50	—
1968-S	—	7.50
1969-D	20.00	—
1969-S	—	7.50
1970-D	40.00	—
1970-S	—	12.00

Clad Composition	MS-65	PF-65
1971	17.50	—
1971-D	12.00	—
1971-S	—	5.00
1972	15.50	—
1972-D	14.50	—
1972-S	—	5.00
1973	20.00	—
1973-D	12.00	—
1973-S	—	5.00
1974	25.00	—
1974-D	17.00	—
1974-S	—	5.00

BICENTENNIAL REVERSE

A variety of coinage proposals for the nation's bicentennial emerged in the years leading up to the celebration. Among them were proposals for special commemorative coins (the U.S. Mint had not issued commemorative coins since 1954), redesigning all six circulating coins, issuing a two-cent coin with a Bicentennial design, and issuing a gold commemorative coin. The Mint and Treasury Department initially resisted any changes to circulating coin designs and the issuance of commemorative coins, but they eased their opposition as the various proposals were winnowed to a final bill that was signed into law Oct. 18, 1973, by President Richard M. Nixon. That bill called for quarters, half dollars, and dollar coins struck after July 4, 1975, to bear new reverse designs emblematic of the nation's Bicentennial. The law also called for the coins to bear the dual date "1776-1976."

The law also authorized the Mint to strike the Bicentennial coins in a 40-percent silver composition for inclusion in three-coin mint and proof sets for sale directly to collectors.

To select designs for the Bicentennial coins, the Mint sponsored a contest open to all U.S. citizens. Seth G. Huntington of Minneapolis had his Independence Hall design selected for the half dollar.

1976 Kennedy half dollar, Bicentennial reverse.

Bicentenniual Reverse	MS-65	PF-65
1976	16.50	—
1976-D	14.00	—
1976-S	—	5.00
40-Percent Silver Composition	MS-65	PF-65
1976-S	12.00	7.50

REGULAR REVERSE RESUMED

Starting in 1992, Kennedy half dollars in the traditional 90-percent silver composition were struck for inclusion in silver proof sets, which also included silver dimes and silver quarters.

Regular Reverse Resumed	MS-65	PF-65
1977	12.50	—
1977-D	16.50	—
1977-S	—	4.50

Regular Reverse Resumed	MS-65	PF-65
1978	12.00	—
1978-D	15.00	—
1978-S	—	5.00
1979	13.50	—
1979-D	13.50	—
1979-S	—	5.00
1980-P	12.50	—
1980-D	17.50	—
1980-S	—	5.00
1981-P	15.00	—
1981-D	20.00	—
1981-S	—	5.00
1982-P	18.50	—
1982-D	20.00	—
1982-S	—	5.00
1983-P	20.00	—
1983-D	12.50	—
1983-S	—	5.00
1984-P	12.00	—
1984-D	18.00	—
1984-S	—	6.00
1985-P	16.50	—
1985-D	12.00	—
1985-S	—	5.00
1986-P	17.50	—
1986-D	14.00	—
1986-S	—	6.00
1987-P	16.50	—
1987-D	12.50	—
1987-S	—	5.00
1988-P	16.50	—
1988-D	10.00	—
1988-S	—	5.00
1989-P	13.00	—
1989-D	13.00	—
1989-S	—	5.00
1990-P	18.00	—
1990-D	20.00	—
1990-S	—	5.00
1991-P	12.50	—
1991-D	16.00	—

Regular Reverse Resumed	MS-65	PF-65
1991-S	—	5.00
1992-P	10.00	—
1992-D	10.00	—
1992-S	—	5.00
1992-S silver	—	11.00
1993-P	12.00	—
1993-D	10.00	—
1993-S	—	5.00
1993-S silver	—	13.00
1994-P	12.00	—
1994-D	8.50	—
1994-S	—	5.00
1994-S silver	—	11.00
1995-P	10.00	—
1995-D	8.00	—
1995-S	—	12.00
1995-S silver	—	46.00
1996-P	10.00	—
1996-D	10.00	—
1996-S	—	9.00
1996-S silver	—	13.00
1997-P	14.00	—
1997-D	13.50	—
1997-S	—	10.00
1997-S silver	—	35.00
1998-P	12.50	—
1998-D	12.50	—
1998-S	—	7.00
1998-S silver	—	11.00
1999-P	11.00	—
1999-D	10.00	—
1999-S	—	8.00
1999-S silver	—	13.00
2000-P	12.00	—
2000-D	12.00	—
2000-S	—	5.00
2000-S silver	—	11.00
2001-P	10.00	—
2001-D	9.00	—
2001-S	—	5.00
2001-S silver	—	11.00

Regular Reverse Resumed	MS-65	PF-65
2002-P	10.00	—
2002-D	10.00	—
2002-S	—	5.00
2002-S silver	—	11.00
2003-P	6.00	—
2003-D	6.00	—
2003-S	—	5.00
2003-S silver	—	11.00
2004-P	4.50	—
2004-D	4.50	—
2004-S	—	6.00
2004-S silver	—	11.00
2005-P	6.00	—
2005-P satin finish	8.00	—
2005-D	5.00	—
2005-D satin finish	10.00	—
2005-S	—	5.00
2005-S silver	—	12.00
2006-P	4.50	—
2006-P satin finish	12.00	—
2006-D	4.50	—
2006-D satin finish	14.00	—
2006-S	—	6.00
2006-S silver	—	12.00
2007-P	4.50	—
2007-P satin finish	8.00	—
2007-D	4.50	—
2007-D satin finish	8.00	—
2007-S	—	6.00
2007-S silver	—	13.50

2004-S Kennedy half dollar.

Regular Reverse Resumed	MS-65	PF-65
2008-P	4.50	—
2008-P satin finish	8.50	—
2008-D	4.50	—
2008-D satin finish	8.50	—
2008-S	—	9.00
2008-S silver	—	12.00
2009-P	4.50	—
2009-P satin finish	8.50	—
2009-S	—	6.00
2009-S silver	—	11.00
2010-P	4.50	—
2010-P satin finish	8.50	—
2010-D	4.50	—
2010-D satin finish	8.50	—
2010-S	—	13.00
2010-S silver	—	12.00
2011-P	4.50	—
2011-D	4.50	—
2011-S	—	9.00
2011-S silver	—	12.00
2012-P	4.50	—
2012-D	4.50	—
2012-S	—	—
2012-S silver	—	—

SEATED LIBERTY DOLLARS

Christian Gobrecht's Seated Liberty design first appeared on a silver dollar in 1836. Gobrecht dollars, as they are commonly called, were also struck in 1838 and 1839, but they saw limited production, and many of the varieties produced during those years are considered patterns. Some restrikes produced in later years also exist.

After a 36-year lapse, production of silver dollars for circulation began again in 1840 using a version of Gobrecht's original 1836 design. The lettered edge used on early silver dollars was replaced by a reeded edge.

1845 Seated Liberty dollar.

	F	XF
1840	340.00	680.00
1841	315.00	610.00
1842	315.00	630.00
1843	315.00	465.00
1844	360.00	785.00
1845	385.00	900.00
1846	345.00	650.00
1846-O	370.00	775.00
1847	315.00	465.00
1848	515.00	1,250.00
1849	350.00	600.00
1850	380.00	1,750.00
1850-O	515.00	1,550.00
1851	5,750.00	18,000.00
1852	5,200.00	15,000.00
1853	550.00	1,100.00
1854	2,000.00	4,500.00
1855	1,500.00	3,750.00
1856	650.00	1,650.00
1857	675.00	1,500.00
1858 proof, restrike	4,000.00	7,250.00
1859	400.00	655.00
1859-O	315.00	465.00
1859-S	515.00	1,550.00
1860	380.00	660.00
1860-O	315.00	465.00
1861	900.00	1,750.00
1862	850.00	1,450.00
1863	575.00	985.00
1864	500.00	920.00
1865	420.00	1,050.00
1866, 2 known	—	—

1871 Seated Liberty dollar with motto above eagle.

Motto Above Eagle	F	XF
1866	440.00	800.00
1867	400.00	670.00
1868	400.00	650.00
1869	370.00	640.00
1870	350.00	600.00
1870-CC	825.00	3,650.00
1870-S, 12-15 known	—	—
1871	330.00	545.00
1871-CC	4,750.00	14,500.00
1872	330.00	500.00
1872-CC	2,850.00	4,850.00
1872-S	550.00	2,000.00
1873	340.00	510.00
1873-CC	11,500.00	31,500.00

TRADE DOLLARS

Trade dollars were struck to facilitate trade with Southeast Asia. They were largely intended to compete against the Mexican peso, which had slightly more silver than a standard dollar, and trade coins of other countries.

The legal-tender status of Trade dollars initially was limited in the United States, but in 1876, when the price of silver dropped, they ceased to be legal tender altogether until their status was restored in 1965. Eighteen million were redeemed by the government in 1887. Only proof examples were struck from 1879 to 1885.

It was common for Asian merchants to impress a character into Trade dollars and other silver coins to confirm that they accepted them as good quality. These "chop marks" are commonly found on Trade dollars; some have several marks. They reduce a coin's value because they are considered mutilation, but some numismatists have researched the marks. Chop-marked Trade dollars are not as valuable as unmarked examples, but they are still collectible.

1876 Trade dollar.

	F	XF
1873	165.00	250.00
1873-CC	330.00	700.00
1873-S	155.00	265.00
1874	150.00	250.00
1874-CC	310.00	600.00
1874-S	160.00	235.00
1875	375.00	590.00
1875-CC	285.00	510.00
1875-S	150.00	225.00
1876	160.00	235.00
1876-CC	300.00	525.00
1875-S	150.00	225.00
1877	160.00	235.00
1877-CC	320.00	700.00
1877-S	150.00	225.00
1878	—	proof 1,300
1878-CC	710.00	2,400.00
1878-S	150.00	225.00
1879	—	proof 1,275
1880	—	proof 1,250
1881	—	proof 1,300
1882	—	proof 1,275
1883	—	proof 1,300
1884	—	proof 100,000
1885 proof, rare	—	—

MORGAN DOLLARS

The Morgan dollar – named for its designer, George T. Morgan – was introduced in response to pressure from silver-mining interests to remove excess silver from the market. For decades, silver dollars were scarce in circulation. With the boom in silver mining, the price of the metal dropped as supplies increased.

The new design marked the reintroduction of circulating silver dollars after a five-year absence. Because they were inconvenient to carry and use, however, perhaps hundreds of thousands of these dollars sat for decades in bags held as private, bank, and government reserves. The U.S. Treasury was stuck with such an excess that thousands remained on hand for almost a century, prompting the famous General Services Administration auction of silver dollars in the 1970s. They were sold in specially made cases, and Morgan dollars in the GSA cases often command a slight premium.

Morgan dollars have long been popular among collectors because of their appealing design, their large size, and the lore of silver dollars. But because large quantities of the coin survived, they remain affordable in nice circulated grades.

Collecting uncirculated Morgan dollars, however, requires a higher level of expertise and a bigger pocketbook. Because of their popularity and subsequent demand, a one-point difference in higher uncirculated grades can be the difference between hundreds or even thousands of dollars in value. That demand is further fueled by those

1887-O Morgan dollar.

who promote Morgan dollars as investments.

Strike quality among Morgan dollars can vary from mint to mint. San Francisco Mint examples are usually fully struck, Philadelphia strikes are of medium quality, and New Orleans dollars are usually the most weakly struck. The differences are most obvious on the eagle's breast.

	VF	MS-60
1878 8 tail feathers	45.00	150.00
1878 7-over-8 tail feathers	45.00	150.00
1878 7 tail feathers, reverse of 1878	45.00	70.00
1878 7 tail feathers, reverse of 1879	45.00	80.00
1878-CC	100.00	245.00
1878-S	35.00	65.00
1879	30.00	55.00
1879-CC	265.00	4,425.00
1879-O	30.00	75.00
1879-S reverse of 1878	40.00	150.00
1879-S reverse of 1879	30.00	55.00
1880	30.00	50.00
1880-CC reverse of 1878	245.00	575.00
1880-CC reverse of 1879	240.00	500.00
1880-O	30.00	70.00
1880-S	30.00	50.00
1881	30.00	55.00
1881-CC	410.00	540.00
1881-O	30.00	50.00
1881-S	30.00	50.00
1882	30.00	50.00
1882-CC	110.00	200.00
1882-O	30.00	55.00
1882-S	30.00	50.00
1883	30.00	50.00
1883-CC	110.00	200.00
1883-O	30.00	45.00
1883-S	35.00	665.00
1884	30.00	50.00
1884-CC	140.00	200.00
1884-O	30.00	45.00
1884-S	35.00	7,500
1885	35.00	45.00

	VF	MS-60
1885-CC	580.00	620.00
1885-O	30.00	45.00
1885-S	40.00	245.00
1886	30.00	45.00
1886-O	35.00	690.00
1886-S	85.00	325.00
1887	35.00	45.00
1887-O	35.00	65.00
1887-S	35.00	130.00
1888	30.00	50.00
1888-O	30.00	50.00
1888-S	210.00	335.00
1889	30.00	50.00
1889-CC	1,200.00	25,500.00
1889-O	35.00	160.00
1889-S	65.00	255.00
1890	30.00	50.00
1890-CC	100.00	440.00
1890-O	35.00	75.00
1890-S	35.00	65.00
1891	35.00	60.00
1891-CC	100.00	390.00
1891-O	35.00	160.00
1891-S	35.00	55.00
1892	40.00	235.00
1892-CC	290.00	8,800.00
1892-O	40.00	235.00
1892-S	135.00	44,500.00
1893	260.00	700.00
1893-CC	625.00	4,175.00
1893-O	380.00	2,600.00
1893-S	5,750.00	130,000.00
1894	1,425.00	3,500.00
1894-O	60.00	715.00

1892-S Morgan dollar.

	VF	MS-60
1894-S	110.00	785.00
1895	proof 36,500	—
1895-O	480.00	15,500.00
1895-S	935.00	3,850.00
1896	30.00	50.00
1896-O	35.00	1,450.00
1896-S	60.00	1,775.00
1897	30.00	50.00
1897-O	35.00	735.00
1897-S	35.00	70.00
1898	30.00	50.00
1898-O	30.00	50.00
1898-S	35.00	270.00
1899	200.00	265.00
1899-O	30.00	50.00
1899-S	35.00	410.00
1900	30.00	50.00
1900-O	30.00	50.00
1900-S	35.00	320.00
1901	60.00	2,450.00
1901-O	35.00	50.00
1901-S	35.00	510.00
1902	35.00	60.00
1902-O	30.00	50.00
1902-S	150.00	360.00
1903	50.00	65.00
1903-O	375.00	410.00
1903-S	215.00	3,950.00
1904	35.00	95.00
1904-O	35.00	55.00
1904-S	90.00	1,600.00
1921	30.00	45.00
1921-D	30.00	50.00
1921-S	30.00	50.00

1901 Morgan dollar.

PEACE DOLLARS

Like the Morgan dollar before it, the Peace dollar was the result of a congressional mandate for a new, large coinage of silver dollars. When the coin-collecting community learned of plans for a new silver dollar, it pushed for a new design to commemorate the end of World War I rather than reviving the Morgan-dollar design. The new design by sculptor Anthony de Francisci depicts a radiant Liberty head on the obverse. The reverse depicts an eagle on a rocky perch above the word "Peace."

Like the Morgan dollar, large numbers of Peace dollars survived, especially in uncirculated grades. Though popular as classic U.S. silver dollars, they are not as popular as Morgan dollars among collectors and investors. As a result, they are more affordable in higher grades.

1921 Peace dollar.

	VF	MS-60
1921	135.00	265.00
1922	30.00	45.00
1922-D	30.00	50.00
1922-S	30.00	50.00
1923	30.00	45.00
1923-D	30.00	60.00
1923-S	30.00	50.00
1924	30.00	45.00
1924-S	35.00	210.00
1925	30.00	45.00
1925-S	35.00	80.00
1926	30.00	55.00
1926-D	30.00	80.00
1926-S	30.00	60.00
1927	35.00	70.00
1927-D	35.00	175.00

	VF	MS-60
1927-S	35.00	180.00
1928	390.00	485.00
1928-S large S	50.00	220.00
1928-S small S	40.00	180.00
1934	45.00	110.00
1934-D	45.00	155.00
1934-S	80.00	1,875.00
1935	45.00	65.00
1935-S	45.00	250.00

EISENHOWER DOLLARS

Dwight D. Eisenhower, supreme commander of the Allied forces in Europe during World War II and the 34th U.S. president, died March 28, 1969. Legislation to again strike a dollar coin, which had not been produced since 1935, was introduced in Congress the following fall. It stated that Eisenhower be honored on the dollar's obverse. The reverse was to be emblematic of the first moon landing, which occurred July 20, 1969.

U.S. Mint Chief Sculptor-Engraver Frank Gasparro designed both sides of the coin. For the reverse, Gasparro fashioned an eagle with an olive branch, a symbol of peace, in its claws landing on the moon with the Earth symbolized as a small orb in the background. The Apollo 11 spacecraft that first landed on the moon was nicknamed "The Eagle."

The Eisenhower dollar legislation also authorized the production of 40-percent silver specimens for inclusion in mint and proof sets.

1974-D Eisenhower dollar.

	MS-63	PF-65
1971	10.00	—
1971-D	8.00	—
1971-S silver	16.00	11.00
1972	18.00	—
1972-D	9.00	—
1972-S silver	16.00	9.00
1973	12.00	—
1973-D	12.00	—
1973-S	—	12.00
1973-S silver	16.00	45.00
1974	15.00	—
1974-D	7.50	—
1974-S	—	11.00
1974-S silver	16.00	11.00

BICENTENNIAL REVERSE

A variety of coinage proposals for the nation's bicentennial emerged in the years leading up to the celebration. Among them were proposals for special commemorative coins (the U.S. Mint had not issued commemorative coins since 1954), redesigning all six circulating coins, issuing a two-cent coin with a Bicentennial design, and issuing a gold commemorative coin. The Mint and Treasury Department initially resisted any changes to circulating coin designs and the issuance of commemorative coins, but they eased their opposition as the various proposals were winnowed to a final bill that was signed into law Oct. 18, 1973, by President Richard M. Nixon. That bill called for quarters, half dollars, and dollar coins struck after July 4, 1975, to bear new reverse designs emblematic of the nation's Bicentennial. The law also called for the coins to bear the dual date "1776-1976."

The law also authorized the Mint to strike the Bicentennial coins in a 40-percent silver composition for inclusion in three-coin uncirculated and proof sets for sale directly to collectors.

To select designs for the Bicentennial coins, the Mint sponsored a contest open to all U.S. citizens. A depiction of the Liberty Bell superimposed over the moon, submitted by Dennis R. Williams of Columbus, Ohio, was selected for the dollar. In 1976 the lettering on the reverse was changed to thinner letters, resulting in Type 1 (thicker letters) and Type 2 (thinner letters) for that year.

1976 Eisenhower dollar with Bicentennial reverse.

Bicentennial Reverse	MS-63	PF-65
1976 Type 1	12.00	—
1976 Type 2	8.00	—
1976-D Type 1	7.50	—
1976-D Type 2	6.00	—
1976-S Type 1	—	10.00
1976-S Type 2	—	9.00
1976-S silver	16.00	14.00
1977	5.00	—
1977-D	4.00	—
1977-S	—	9.00
1978	4.00	—
1978-D	4.75	—
1978-S	—	9.00

CLASSIC HEAD GOLD $2.50

Coinage reform legislation passed in 1834 increased the gold-to-silver value ratio in the U.S. bimetallic monetary system from 15-to-1 to 16.002-to-1. Thus, the fineness and gold content of the $2.50 decreased.

A new rendering of Liberty appeared on the obverse; minor design modifications appeared on the reverse.

1838 Classic Head gold $2.50.

Classic Head	VF	XF
1834	475.00	675.00
1835	475.00	675.00
1836	475.00	675.00
1837	500.00	800.00
1838	500.00	625.00
1838-C	1,700.00	3,000.00
1839	500.00	900.00
1839-C	1,500.00	2,650.00
1839-D	1,750.00	3,450.00
1839-O	700.00	1,100.00

CORONET GOLD $2.50

Legislation passed in 1837 set the fineness of all U.S. gold and silver coins at 0.9000 and revised the gold-to-silver value ratio to 15.998-to-1. Thus, the size and actual gold weight of the $2.50 coin changed slightly in 1840.

A new image of Liberty, which emulated the one used on higher-denomination gold coins of the time, appeared on the obverse. With some modification, the basic reverse design used since 1808 was retained.

Coronet	F	XF
1840	160.00	900.00
1840-C	975.00	1,600.00
1840-D	2,000.00	8,700.00
1840-O	250.00	825.00
1841	—	85,000.00
1841-C	750.00	2,000.00
1841-D	950.00	4,750.00
1842	500.00	2,600.00
1842-C	700.00	3,500.00

Coronet	F	XF
1842-D	900.00	4,000.00
1842-O	240.00	1,200.00
1843	160.00	450.00
1843-C	800.00	2,200.00
1843-D	920.00	2,350.00
1843-O	165.00	250.00
1844	225.00	850.00
1844-C	700.00	2,600.00
1844-D	785.00	2,200.00
1845	190.00	350.00
1845-D	950.00	2,600.00
1845-O	550.00	2,300.00
1846	200.00	500.00
1846-C	725.00	3,500.00
1846-D	800.00	2,000.00
1846-O	170.00	400.00
1847	140.00	360.00
1847-C	900.00	2,300.00
1847-D	800.00	2,250.00
1847-O	165.00	400.00
1848	315.00	850.00
1848-C	800.00	2,100.00
1848-D	1,000.00	2,500.00
1849	180.00	475.00
1849-C	800.00	2,150.00
1849-D	950.00	2,500.00
1850	265.00	360.00
1850-C	800.00	2,000.00
1850-D	950.00	2,350.00
1850-O	300.00	485.00
1851	265.00	330.00
1851-C	900.00	2,250.00
1851-D	1,000.00	2,500.00
1851-O	300.00	370.00
1852	265.00	330.00
1852-C	975.00	2,100.00
1852-D	1,100.00	2,950.00
1852-O	300.00	365.00
1853	265.00	330.00
1853-D	1,250.00	3,450.00
1854	265.00	330.00

Coronet	F	XF
1854-C	1,100.00	2,450.00
1854-D	2,100.00	6,950.00
1854-O	300.00	365.00
1854-S	95,000.00	300,000.00
1855	270.00	335.00
1855-C	1,050.00	3,250.00
1855-D	2,100.00	7,500.00
1856	270.00	335.00
1856-C	985.00	2,500.00
1856-D	3,850.00	12,850.00
1856-O	300.00	750.00
1856-S	300.00	425.00
1857	270.00	335.00
1857-D	1,025.00	2,775.00
1857-O	300.00	425.00
1857-S	300.00	365.00
1858	275.00	340.00
1858-C	965.00	2,100.00
1859	275.00	350.00
1859-D	1,150.00	3,100.00
1859-S	310.00	950.00
1860	275.00	340.00
1860-C	985.00	2,175.00
1860-S	310.00	625.00
1861	270.00	335.00
1861-S	320.00	900.00
1862	310.00	600.00
1862-S	650.00	2,100.00
1863 rare	—	—
1863-S	465.00	1,500.00
1864	3,750.00	11,500.00
1865	2,950.00	7,750.00
1865-S	320.00	600.00
1866	775.00	3,150.00
1866-S	365.00	625.00
1867	350.00	850.00
1867-S	300.00	575.00
1868	300.00	400.00
1868-S	270.00	365.00
1869	300.00	435.00
1869-S	300.00	445.00

Coronet	F	XF
1870	290.00	550.00
1870-S	270.00	465.00
1871	300.00	385.00
1871-S	270.00	415.00
1872	300.00	800.00
1872-S	275.00	485.00
1873	270.00	365.00
1873-S	280.00	400.00
1874	285.00	425.00
1875	1,950.00	5,500.00
1875-S	270.00	375.00
1876	285.00	675.00
1876-S	285.00	625.00
1877	310.00	875.00
1877-S	265.00	355.00
1878	265.00	345.00
1878-S	265.00	345.00
1879	270.00	355.00
1879-S	270.00	365.00
1880	275.00	385.00
1881	950.00	3,150.00
1882	270.00	375.00
1883	280.00	750.00
1884	275.00	440.00
1885	400.00	1,850.00
1886	275.00	375.00
1887	275.00	365.00
1888	270.00	365.00
1889	270.00	365.00
1890	375.00	365.00
1891	275.00	365.00
1892	275.00	365.00
1893	270.00	355.00
1894	275.00	365.00
1895	265.00	355.00
1896	265.00	350.00
1897	270.00	350.00
1898	265.00	345.00
1899	265.00	345.00
1900	265.00	345.00
1901	265.00	345.00

Coronet	F	XF
1902	265.00	345.00
1903	265.00	345.00
1904	265.00	345.00
1905	265.00	345.00
1906	265.00	345.00
1907	265.00	345.00

INDIAN HEAD GOLD $2.50

A new design by Bela Lyon Pratt replaced the long-running Coronet Head in 1908 on the gold $2.50. Its intaglio features were unusual and controversial. Some feared the incuse design would allow dirt and germs to accumulate in the coin's recesses. From a collector's standpoint, however, the technique shielded the coin from wear.

Legislation passed April 11, 1930, discontinued the gold $2.50.

1911 Indian Head gold $2.50.

Indian Head	VF	AU
1908	255.00	310.00
1909	255.00	310.00
1910	255.00	310.00
1911	255.00	310.00
1911-D	1,150.00	2,850.00
1912	255.00	315.00
1913	255.00	310.00
1914	260.00	370.00
1914-D	255.00	320.00
1915	255.00	300.00
1925-D	255.00	300.00
1926	255.00	300.00
1927	255.00	300.00
1928	255.00	300.00
1929	255.00	320.00

CLASSIC HEAD GOLD $5

Coinage reform legislation passed in 1834 increased the gold-to-silver value ratio in the U.S. bimetallic monetary system from 15-to-1 to 16.002-to-1. Thus, the fineness and gold content of the $5 decreased. The value of the gold content of the previous $5 coins had exceeded their face value.

Obverse and reverse designs were also modified slightly. Most notably, the motto "E Pluribus Unum" was removed from the reverse to distinguish the new coins from the old ones.

1834 Classic Head gold $5.

Classic Head	VF	XF
1834 plain 4	550.00	790.00
1834 crosslet 4	1,650.00	2,900.00
1835	550.00	790.00
1836	550.00	790.00
1837	550.00	790.00
1838	550.00	890.00
1838-C	2,550.00	5,500.00
1838-D	2,100.00	4,650.00

CORONET GOLD $5

Legislation passed in 1837 set the fineness of all U.S. gold and silver coins at 0.9000 and revised the gold-to-silver value ratio to 15.998-to-1. Thus, the diameter and actual gold weight of the $5 coin changed slightly in 1839.

A new image of Liberty appeared on the obverse. With some modification, the basic reverse design used since 1807 was retained. A congressional act passed March 3, 1865, allowed the addition of the motto "In God We Trust" to all U.S. gold and silver coins.

1841 Coronet gold $5.

Coronet	VF	XF
1839	560.00	590.00
1839-C	2,300.00	2,900.00
1839-D	2,200.00	3,200.00
1840	550.00	570.00
1840-C	2,200.00	3,000.00
1840-D	2,200.00	3,000.00
1840-O	580.00	610.00
1841	560.00	590.00
1841-C	1,850.00	2,400.00
1841-D	1,800.00	2,350.00
1841-O, 2 known	—	—
1842 small letters	345.00	1,100.00
1842 large letters	750.00	2,000.00
1842-C	1,800.00	2,200.00
1842-D small date	2,000.00	2,300.00
1842-D large date	2,350.00	6,500.00
1842-O	1,000.00	3,400.00
1843	550.00	580.00
1843-C	1,850.00	2,500.00
1843-D	1,950.00	2,600.00
1843-O small letters	580.00	1,700.00
1843-O large letters	585.00	1,175.00
1844	550.00	580.00
1844-C	1,900.00	3,000.00
1844-D	1,950.00	2,400.00
1844-O	585.00	590.00
1845	550.00	580.00
1845-D	1,900.00	2,400.00
1845-O	415.00	800.00
1846	550.00	580.00
1846-C	1,900.00	3,000.00
1846-D	1,800.00	2,400.00
1846-O	375.00	1,000.00
1847	550.00	580.00
1847-C	1,800.00	2,400.00

Coronet	VF	XF
1847-D	2,000.00	2,500.00
1847-O	2,200.00	6,750.00
1848	550.00	580.00
1848-C	1,900.00	2,250.00
1848-D	2,000.00	2,350.00
1849	550.00	580.00
1849-C	1,900.00	2,400.00
1849-D	2,000.00	2,600.00
1850	550.00	580.00
1850-C	1,850.00	2,300.00
1850-D	1,950.00	2,500.00
1851	550.00	580.00
1851-C	1,900.00	2,350.00
1851-D	1,950.00	2,400.00
1851-O	600.00	1,500.00
1852	550.00	580.00
1852-C	1,900.00	2,450.00
1852-D	2,000.00	2,450.00
1853	550.00	580.00
1853-C	1,950.00	2,350.00
1853-D	2,000.00	2,500.00
1854	550.00	580.00
1854-C	1,900.00	2,300.00
1854-D	1,875.00	2,200.00
1854-O	580.00	610.00
1854-S, rare	—	—
1855	550.00	580.00
1855-C	1,900.00	2,300.00
1855-D	1,950.00	2,400.00
1855-O	675.00	2,100.00
1855-S	390.00	1,000.00
1856	550.00	580.00
1856-C	1,875.00	2,400.00
1856-D	1,950.00	2,600.00
1856-O	650.00	1,600.00
1856-S	300.00	590.00
1857	550.00	580.00
1857-C	1,900.00	2,500.00
1857-D	2,000.00	2,650.00
1857-O	640.00	1,400.00
1857-S	560.00	590.00

Coronet	VF	XF
1858	560.00	590.00
1858-C	1,900.00	2,350.00
1858-D	2,000.00	2,450.00
1858-S	825.00	2,350.00
1859	560.00	590.00
1859-C	1,900.00	2,450.00
1859-D	2,150.00	2,600.00
1859-S	1,800.00	4,150.00
1860	560.00	590.00
1860-C	2,100.00	3,000.00
1860-D	1,900.00	2,600.00
1860-S	1,100.00	2,100.00
1861	550.00	590.00
1861-C	2,400.00	3,900.00
1861-D	4,700.00	7,000.00
1861-S	1,100.00	4,500.00
1862	800.00	1,850.00
1862-S	3,000.00	6,000.00
1863	1,200.00	3,750.00
1863-S	1,450.00	4,100.00
1864	650.00	1,850.00
1864-S	4,750.00	16,000.00
1865	1,450.00	4,100.00
1865-S	1,400.00	2,400.00
1866-S	1,750.00	4,000.00

Coronet, Motto Above Eagle	VF	XF
1866	750.00	1,650.00
1866-S	900.00	2,600.00
1867	500.00	1,500.00
1867-S	1,400.00	2,900.00
1868	650.00	1,000.00
1868-S	485.00	1,550.00
1869	925.00	2,400.00
1869-S	500.00	1,750.00
1870	800.00	2,000.00
1870-CC	5,250.00	15,000.00
1870-S	950.00	2,600.00
1871	900.00	1,700.00
1871-CC	1,250.00	3,000.00
1871-S	500.00	950.00
1872	850.00	1,925.00

Coronet, Motto Above Eagle	VF	XF
1872-CC	1,250.00	5,000.00
1872-S	535.00	800.00
1873 closed 3	470.00	485.00
1873 open 3	465.00	475.00
1873-CC	2,600.00	12,500.00
1873-S	525.00	1,400.00
1874	660.00	1,675.00
1874-CC	850.00	1,700.00
1874-S	640.00	2,100.00
1875	34,000.00	45,000.00
1875-CC	1,400.00	4,500.00
1875-S	715.00	2,250.00
1876	1,100.00	2,500.00
1876-CC	1,450.00	5,000.00
1876-S	2,000.00	3,600.00
1877	900.00	2,750.00
1877-CC	1,000.00	3,300.00
1877-S	500.00	650.00
1878	470.00	480.00
1878-CC	3,100.00	7,200.00
1878-S	465.00	475.00
1879	465.00	475.00
1879-CC	1,000.00	1,500.00
1879-S	470.00	480.00
1880	460.00	470.00
1880-CC	625.00	815.00
1880-S	460.00	470.00
1881	460.00	470.00
1881-CC	650.00	1,500.00
1881-S	460.00	470.00
1882	460.00	470.00
1882-CC	625.00	675.00
1882-S	460.00	470.00
1883	480.00	490.00
1883-CC	625.00	1,100.00

1882 gold $5 with motto above eagle.

Coronet, Motto Above Eagle	VF	XF
1883-S	480.00	500.00
1884	480.00	500.00
1884-CC	625.00	975.00
1884-S	480.00	490.00
1885	460.00	470.00
1885-S	460.00	470.00
1886	460.00	470.00
1886-S	460.00	470.00
1887	—	14,500.00
1887-S	460.00	470.00
1888	480.00	485.00
1888-S	465.00	475.00
1889	575.00	585.00
1890	500.00	510.00
1890-CC	575.00	585.00
1891	470.00	480.00
1891-CC	560.00	565.00
1892	460.00	470.00
1892-CC	560.00	585.00
1892-O	525.00	1,000.00
1892-S	460.00	470.00
1893	460.00	470.00
1893-CC	600.00	635.00
1893-O	475.00	580.00
1893-S	460.00	470.00
1894	460.00	470.00
1894-O	480.00	490.00
1894-S	490.00	525.00
1895	460.00	470.00
1895-S	470.00	490.00
1896	460.00	470.00
1896-S	470.00	480.00
1897	460.00	470.00
1897-S	460.00	470.00
1898	460.00	470.00
1898-S	460.00	470.00
1899	460.00	470.00
1899-S	460.00	470.00
1900	460.00	470.00
1900-S	460.00	470.00
1901	460.00	470.00

Coronet, Motto Above Eagle	VF	XF
1901-S	460.00	470.00
1902	460.00	470.00
1902-S	460.00	470.00
1903	460.00	470.00
1903-S	460.00	470.00
1904	460.00	470.00
1904-S	470.00	480.00
1905	460.00	470.00
1905-S	460.00	470.00
1906	460.00	470.00
1906-D	460.00	470.00
1906-S	460.00	470.00
1907	460.00	470.00
1907-D	460.00	470.00
1908	460.00	470.00

INDIAN HEAD GOLD $5

A new design by Bela Lyon Pratt replaced the long-running Coronet Head in 1908 on the gold $5. Its intaglio features were unusual and controversial. Some feared the incuse design would allow dirt and germs to accumulate in the coin's recesses. From a collector's standpoint, however, the technique shielded the coin from wear.

The Gold Reserve Act of Jan. 30, 1934, discontinued all U.S. gold coinage.

1929 Indian Head gold $5.

Indian Head	VF	XF
1908	520.00	530.00
1908-D	520.00	530.00
1908-S	595.00	605.00
1909	520.00	530.00
1909-D	520.00	530.00
1909-O	3,950.00	4,850.00
1909-S	550.00	570.00

Indian Head	VF	XF
1910	520.00	530.00
1910-D	520.00	530.00
1910-S	560.00	585.00
1911	520.00	530.00
1911-D	600.00	775.00
1911-S	530.00	565.00
1912	520.00	530.00
1912-S	565.00	595.00
1913	520.00	530.00
1913-S	560.00	590.00
1914	520.00	530.00
1914-D	520.00	530.00
1914-S	565.00	585.00
1915	520.00	530.00
1915-S	575.00	600.00
1916-S	545.00	565.00
1929	11,000.00	14,250.00

CORONET GOLD $10

The discovery of gold in Southern states and later in California prompted the resumption of $10 coin production in 1838 after a 34-year lapse. Legislation passed in 1837 set the fineness of all U.S. gold and silver coins at 0.9000 and revised the gold-to-silver ratio to 15.998-to-1. Thus, the diameter and actual gold weight of the new $10 coin decreased from the previous issue.

The new obverse design, by Christian Gobrecht, featured a portrait of Liberty facing left and wearing a coronet. The reverse featured a new eagle design and, for the first time, the denomination, designated as "Ten D.". In 1839, some minor redesign of Liberty on the obverse resulted in the image being tilted backward. A congressional act passed March 3, 1865, allowed the addition of the motto "In God We Trust" to all U.S. gold and silver coins.

1839 Coronet gold $10, old-style head.

Coronet, Old-Style Head	F	VF
1838	1,750.00	2,650.00
1839	1,000.00	1,250.00

Coronet, New-Style Head	VF	XF
1839	1,550.00	6,850.00
1840	1,060.00	1,335.00
1841	1,050.00	1,235.00
1841-O	3,450.00	6,950.00
1842	1,050.00	1,160.00
1842-O	1,060.00	1,465.00
1843	1,050.00	1,265.00
1843-O	1,060.00	1,220.00
1844	1,350.00	3,200.00
1844-O	1,060.00	1,400.00
1845	1,220.00	1,345.00
1845-O	1,060.00	1,335.00
1846	1,100.00	1,250.00
1846-O	1,060.00	1,150.00
1847	1,050.00	1,100.00
1847-O	1,050.00	1,100.00
1848	1,050.00	1,160.00
1848-O	1,240.00	1,850.00
1849	1,050.00	1,100.00
1849-O	1,240.00	2,450.00
1850 large date	1,050.00	1,100.00
1850 small date	1,240.00	2,150.00
1850-O	1,075.00	1,275.00
1851	1,050.00	1,100.00
1851-O	1,060.00	1,150.00
1852	1,050.00	1,100.00
1852-O	1,220.00	1,650.00
1853	1,060.00	1,100.00
1853-O	1,075.00	1,160.00
1854	1,050.00	1,120.00
1854-O small date	1,075.00	1,400.00
1854-O large date	1,215.00	2,000.00

1856 Coronet gold $10,
new-style head.

Coronet, New-Style Head	VF	XF
1854-S	1,050.00	1,120.00
1855	1,050.00	1,100.00
1855-O	1,075.00	2,100.00
1856	1,050.00	1,100.00
1856-O	1,375.00	2,150.00
1856-S	1,050.00	1,170.00
1857	1,075.00	1,150.00
1857-O	1,800.00	3,650.00
1857-S	1,060.00	1,100.00
1858	5,200.00	8,250.00
1858-O	1,050.00	1,420.00
1858-S	1,600.00	3,950.00
1859	1,075.00	1,280.00
1859-O	4,250.00	10,500.00
1859-S	2,600.00	5,250.00
1860	1,115.00	1,330.00
1860-O	1,215.00	1,850.00
1860-S	2,950.00	6,400.00
1861	1,050.00	1,100.00
1861-S	1,600.00	3,750.00
1862	1,200.00	1,300.00
1862-S	2,000.00	3,450.00
1863	4,000.00	10,000.00
1863-S	1,600.00	3,750.00
1864	1,800.00	4,950.00
1864-S	5,100.00	17,500.00
1865	1,950.00	4,850.00
1865-S	4,850.00	12,500.00
1866-S	2,650.00	5,950.00
Coronet, Motto Above Eagle	VF	XF
1866	850.00	2,450.00
1866-S	1,550.00	3,850.00
1867	1,500.00	2,600.00
1867-S	2,350.00	6,650.00
1868	1,000.00	1,100.00

1876 Coronet gold $10,
motto above eagle.

Coronet, Motto Above Eagle	VF	XF
1868-S	1,350.00	2,400.00
1869	1,550.00	3,000.00
1869-S	1,500.00	2,700.00
1870	985.00	1,650.00
1870-CC	13,000.00	30,000.00
1870-S	1,150.00	2,850.00
1871	1,500.00	3,000.00
1871-CC	2,600.00	6,400.00
1871-S	1,300.00	2,200.00
1872	2,400.00	5,500.00
1872-CC	2,850.00	9,850.00
1872-S	850.00	1,175.00
1873	4,500.00	9,750.00
1873-CC	6,000.00	13,500.00
1873-S	1,150.00	2,850.00
1874	935.00	965.00
1874-CC	1,150.00	3,650.00
1874-S	1,275.00	3,400.00
1875	40,000.00	67,500.00
1875-CC	4,250.00	9,850.00
1876	3,000.00	8,500.00
1876-CC	3,600.00	7,750.00
1876-S	1,300.00	2,950.00
1877	3,350.00	6,350.00
1877-CC	2,400.00	6,750.00
1877-S	935.00	1,250.00
1878	925.00	965.00
1878-CC	3,850.00	10,000.00
1878-S	935.00	975.00
1879	930.00	965.00
1879-CC	6,650.00	12,500.00
1879-O	2,150.00	5,450.00
1879-S	930.00	965.00
1880	910.00	930.00
1880-CC	900.00	1,000.00

Coronet, Motto Above Eagle	VF	XF
1880-O	1,030.00	1,450.00
1880-S	910.00	930.00
1881	910.00	930.00
1881-CC	1,055.00	1,200.00
1881-O	1,000.00	1,150.00
1881-S	910.00	930.00
1882	910.00	930.00
1882-CC	985.00	1,750.00
1882-O	940.00	1,115.00
1882-S	940.00	965.00
1883	910.00	930.00
1883-CC	1,110.00	1,250.00
1883-O	3,000.00	7,950.00
1883-S	940.00	965.00
1884	940.00	965.00
1884-CC	1,130.00	1,450.00
1884-S	910.00	930.00
1885	910.00	930.00
1885-S	910.00	930.00
1886	910.00	930.00
1886-S	910.00	930.00
1887	940.00	965.00
1887-S	910.00	930.00
1888	940.00	965.00
1888-O	940.00	965.00
1888-S	910.00	930.00
1889	965.00	1,155.00
1889-S	910.00	930.00
1890	950.00	965.00
1890-CC	1,050.00	1,150.00
1891	965.00	1,000.00
1891-CC	1,050.00	1,100.00
1892	910.00	930.00
1892-CC	1,050.00	1,100.00
1892-O	965.00	970.00
1892-S	935.00	990.00
1893	910.00	930.00
1893-CC	1,050.00	1,150.00
1893-O	935.00	965.00
1893-S	935.00	965.00
1894	910.00	930.00

Coronet, Motto Above Eagle	VF	XF
1894-O	935.00	965.00
1894-S	935.00	990.00
1895	910.00	930.00
1895-O	935.00	970.00
1895-S	935.00	980.00
1896	910.00	930.00
1896-S	935.00	960.00
1897	910.00	930.00
1897-O	935.00	970.00
1897-S	935.00	960.00
1898	910.00	930.00
1898-S	935.00	960.00
1899	910.00	930.00
1899-S	910.00	930.00
1899-O	935.00	965.00
1900	910.00	930.00
1900-S	935.00	965.00
1901	910.00	930.00
1901-O	935.00	965.00
1901-S	910.00	930.00
1902	910.00	930.00
1902-S	910.00	930.00
1903	910.00	930.00
1903-O	935.00	965.00
1903-S	910.00	930.00
1904	910.00	930.00
1904-D	935.00	965.00
1905	910.00	930.00
1905-S	935.00	960.00
1906	910.00	930.00
1906-D	910.00	930.00
1906-O	935.00	965.00
1906-S	935.00	960.00
1907	910.00	930.00
1907-D	910.00	930.00
1907-S	935.00	960.00

INDIAN HEAD GOLD $10

Sculptor Augustus Saint-Gaudens designed President Theodore Roosevelt's inaugural medal. Roosevelt liked the result so much that he commissioned the sculptor to improve the design of U.S. coinage. The results included a striking new design, featuring Liberty in an Indian head-dress, for the gold $10 coin in 1907. The coin's smooth edge has 46 stars on it, one for each state in the Union at the time. Two more stars were added in 1912. Congressional acts of March 3, 1865, and Feb. 12, 1873, allowed the motto "In God We Trust" to be placed on U.S. coins but did not mandate it. According to author Don Taxay, Roosevelt considered it sacrilege to use a religious motto on coinage. When the new 1907 gold $10 and $20 coins appeared without the motto, Congress passed legislation on May 18, 1908, mandating its use on all coins on which it had previously appeared.

The Gold Reserve Act of Jan. 30, 1934, discontinued production of all U.S. gold coinage.

1907 Indian Head gold $10.

Indian Head	VF	XF
1907 wire edge	13,850.00	17,500.00
1907 rolled edge	26,000.00	38,500.00
1907 no periods in "E Pluribus Unum"	1,000.00	1,030.00
1908	990.00	1,015.00
1908-D	990.00	1,015.00

1930-S Indian Head
gold $10.

Indian Head, Motto Left of Eagle	VF	XF
1908	990.00	1,000.00
1908-D	990.00	1,030.00
1908-S	1,000.00	1,065.00
1909	985.00	1,000.00
1909-D	990.00	1,015.00
1909-S	990.00	1,015.00
1910	985.00	1,000.00
1910-D	980.00	1,000.00
1910-S	990.00	1,015.00
1911	980.00	1,000.00
1911-D	1,050.00	1,200.00
1911-S	1,020.00	1,040.00
1912	985.00	1,000.00
1912-S	990.00	1,015.00
1913	985.00	1,000.00
1913-S	1,035.00	1,060.00
1914	985.00	1,000.00
1914-D	985.00	1,000.00
1914-S	995.00	1,020.00
1915	985.00	1,000.00
1915-S	1,035.00	1,075.00
1916-S	1,020.00	1,045.00
1920-S	12,500.00	16,850.00
1926	980.00	1,000.00
1930-S	8,500.00	11,250.00
1932	980.00	1,000.00
1933	—	140,000.00

FIRST SPOUSES GOLD $10

The Presidential Dollar Coin Act of 2005 also authorized the minting of half-ounce gold $10 bullion coins
honoring the wives of U.S. presidents. The women will
be honored in the order in which they served, and the

release schedule parallels the release schedule for the Presidential Dollars.

Obverse designs will include the name and likeness of the first spouse, the years during which her husband was president, and a number indicating the order in which her husband served. Reverse images will be emblematic of the spouse's life and work.

For presidents who were not married during their terms in office, the obverse design will include an image of Liberty as depicted on a U.S. coin that circulated during the president's term. Reverse designs will be based on "themes of such President" being honored.

An exception will be the coin for President Chester A. Arthur. The legislation mandates that the obverse depict Alice Paul, a leader in the women's suffrage movement. Paul was born Jan. 11, 1885, during Arthur's term. The reverse design will also represent the suffrage movement.

The First Spouse coins contain a half-ounce of 24-karat gold (.9999 fine).

Washington	MS-65	PF-65
2007-W	630.00	630.00

A. Adams	MS-65	PF-65
2007-W	680.00	680.00

Jefferson	MS-65	PF-65
2007-W	630.00	630.00
Madison	**MS-65**	**PF-65**
2007-W	680.00	680.00

Monroe	MS-65	PF-65
2008-W	975.00	950.00
L. Adams	**MS-65**	**PF-65**
2008-W	1,175.00	1,125.00

Jackson	MS-65	PF-65
2008-W	1,575.00	1,325.00

Van Buren	MS-65	PF-65
2008-W	1,500.00	1,525.00

A. Harrison	MS-65	PF-65
2009-W	1,225.00	1,150.00

L. Tyler	MS-65	PF-65
2009-W	1,525.00	1,325.00

J. Tyler	MS-65	PF-65
2009-W	1,650.00	1,800.00

Polk	MS-65	PF-65
2009-W	1,300.00	1,100.00

Taylor	MS-65	PF-65
2009-W	1,050.00	1,225.00

Fillmore	MS-65	PF-65
2010-W	1,300.00	1,025.00

Pierce	MS-65	PF-65
2010-W	1,000.00	1,225.00

Buchanan	MS-65	PF-65
2010-W	1,000.00	1,075.00

Lincoln	MS-65	PF-65
2010-W	1,000.00	975.00

E. Johnson	MS-65	PF-65
2011-W	1,075.00	1,075.00
Grant	**MS-65**	**PF-65**
2011-W	1,075.00	1,075.00

Hayes	MS-65	PF-65
2011-W	1,325.00	1,075.00
Garfield	**MS-65**	**PF-65**
2011-W	1,325.00	1,075.00

Paul	MS-65	PF-65
2012-W	1,050.00	1,075.00

Cleveland 1	MS-65	PF-65
2012-W	1,050.00	1,075.00

C. Harrison	MS-65	PF-65
2012-W	1,050.00	1,075.00

Cleveland 2	MS-65	PF-65
2012-W	1,050.00	1,075

2013	MS-65	MS-65
Ida McKinley	800.00	825.00
Edith Roosevelt	800.00	825.00
Helen Taft	800.00	825.00
Ellen Wilson, Edith Wilson	800.00	825.00

2014	MS-65	MS-65
Florence Harding	800.00	825.00
Grace Coolidge	800.00	825.00
Lou Hoover	800.00	825.00
Anna Eleanor Roosevelt	800.00	825.00

2015		
Elizabeth Truman		
Mamie Eisenhower		
Jacqueline Kennedy		
Claudia Taylor "Lady Bird" Johnson		

2016		
Patricia Ryan "Pat" Nixon		

LIBERTY GOLD $20

An amendment authorizing a gold $20 coin, or "double eagle," was added to proposed congressional legislation authorizing a gold dollar coin. It passed March 3, 1849. Both coins were advanced by gold interests after the discovery of the precious metal in California in 1848.

James B. Longacre's design for the coin depicts Liberty wearing a coronet, similar to the gold $5 and $10 coins of the same era. The obverse depicts a majestic heraldic eagle with a circle of stars and a radiant arc above it. A congressional act passed March 3, 1865, allowed the addition of the motto "In God We Trust" to all U.S. gold and silver coins. In 1877, the reverse design was modified so the denomination read "Twenty Dollars" instead of "Twenty D."

Liberty	VF	XF
1849, 1 known	—	—
1850	1,945.00	2,025.00
1850-O	1,880.00	3,500.00
1851	1,985.00	2,155.00
1851-O	2,060.00	2,855.00
1852	1,985.00	2,155.00
1852-O	2,015.00	2,650.00
1853	1,985.00	2,155.00
1853-O	2,075.00	3,650.00
1854	1,985.00	2,155.00
1854-O	95,000.00	225,000.00
1854-S	2,065.00	2,145.00
1855	1,985.00	2,145.00
1855-O	3,650.00	19,500.00
1855-S	1,965.00	2,155.00
1856	1,985.00	2,155.00
1856-O	97,500.00	165,000.00
1856-S	1,965.00	2,155.00
1857	1,985.00	2,155.00
1857-O	2,040.00	2,950.00
1857-S	1,965.00	2,155.00
1858	2,040.00	2,145.00
1858-O	2,250.00	3,850.00

1856-S Liberty
gold $20.

Liberty	VF	XF
1858-S	1,965.00	2,175.00
1859	2,040.00	2,450.00
1859-O	6,400.00	16,500.00
1859-S	1,965.00	2,155.00
1860	1,965.00	2,155.00
1860-O	3,650.00	14,500.00
1860-S	1,985.00	2,445.00
1861	1,965.00	2,155.00
1861-O	5,650.00	17,500.00
1861-S	1,985.00	2,250.00
1862	1,965.00	3,500.00
1862-S	1,950.00	2,030.00
1863	1,965.00	2,650.00
1863-S	1,950.00	2,110.00
1864	1,965.00	2,045.00
1864-S	1,950.00	2,090.00
1865	1,965.00	2,110.00
1865-S	1,950.00	2,110.00
1866-S	2,750.00	11,500.00

1867 gold $20,
motto above eagle.

Liberty, Motto Above Eagle	VF	XF
1866	1,910.00	2,075.00
1866-S	1,910.00	2,085.00
1867	1,910.00	2,100.00
1867-S	1,910.00	2,085.00
1868	1,950.00	2,185.00
1868-S	1,910.00	2,055.00
1869	1,920.00	2,045.00
1869-S	1,910.00	2,075.00
1870	1,930.00	2,075.00

Liberty, Motto Above Eagle	VF	XF
1870-CC	200,000.00	275,000.00
1870-S	1,910.00	2,030.00
1871	1,920.00	2,030.00
1871-CC	9,500.00	19,500.00
1871-S	1,910.00	2,045.00
1872	1,910.00	2,075.00
1872-CC	2,550.00	5,450.00
1872-S	1,910.00	2,075.00
1873 closed 3	1,910.00	2,135.00
1873 open 3	1,910.00	2,075.00
1873-CC	2,900.00	4,750.00
1873-S closed 3	1,910.00	2,045.00
1873-S open 3	1,910.00	2,075.00
1874	1,910.00	2,075.00
1874-CC	2,100.00	2,450.00
1874-S	1,910.00	2,045.00
1875	1,910.00	2,075.00
1875-CC	1,950.00	2,250.00
1875-S	1,910.00	2,045.00
1876	1,910.00	2,065.00
1876-CC	1,960.00	2,300.00
1876-S	1,910.00	2,045.00

1877 gold $20, "Twenty Dollars" on reverse.

Liberty, "Twenty Dollars" on Reverse	VF	XF
1877	1,830.00	1,970.00
1877-CC	1,985.00	2,150.00
1877-S	1,820.00	1,870.00
1878	1,840.00	1,970.00
1878-CC	2,450.00	3,950.00
1878-S	1,820.00	1,845.00
1879	1,900.00	1,970.00
1879-CC	3,000.00	4,850.00
1879-O	12,500.00	21,500.00
1879-S	1,820.00	1,845.00
1880	1,930.00	2,000.00
1880-S	1,820.00	1,845.00

Liberty, "Twenty Dollars" on Reverse	VF	XF
1881	12,500.00	21,000.00
1881-S	1,820.00	1,845.00
1882	13,500.00	39,500.00
1882-CC	1,970.00	2,000.00
1882-S	1,820.00	1,845.00
1883	—	proof 27,500
1883-CC	1,970.00	2,000.00
1883-S	1,820.00	1,845.00
1884	—	proof 35,000
1884-CC	1,970.00	2,000.00
1884-S	1,820.00	1,845.00
1885	8,450.00	13,850.00
1885-CC	2,500.00	3,850.00
1885-S	1,820.00	1,845.00
1886	10,500.00	18,500.00
1887	—	AU 26,500
1887-S	1,820.00	1,845.00
1888	1,820.00	1,845.00
1888-S	1,820.00	1,845.00
1889	1,980.00	2,100.00
1889-CC	1,970.00	2,150.00
1889-S	1,820.00	1,845.00
1890	1,820.00	1,870.00
1890-CC	1,970.00	2,000.00
1890-S	1,820.00	1,845.00
1891	8,500.00	15,000.00
1891-CC	4,950.00	9,000.00
1891-S	1,820.00	1,845.00
1892	2,000.00	3,650.00
1892-CC	1,970.00	2,100.00
1892-S	1,820.00	1,845.00
1893	1,820.00	1,865.00
1893-CC	2,070.00	2,100.00
1893-S	1,780.00	1,800.00
1894	1,780.00	1,800.00
1894-S	1,780.00	1,800.00
1895	1,780.00	1,800.00
1895-S	1,780.00	1,800.00
1896	1,780.00	1,800.00
1896-S	1,780.00	1,800.00
1897	1,780.00	1,800.00

Liberty, "Twenty Dollars" on Reverse	VF	XF
1897-S	1,780.00	1,800.00
1898	1,785.00	1,830.00
1898-S	1,785.00	1,800.00
1899	1,780.00	1,800.00
1899-S	1,780.00	1,800.00
1900	1,780.00	1,800.00
1900-S	1,780.00	1,800.00
1901	1,780.00	1,800.00
1901-S	1,780.00	1,800.00
1902	1,780.00	2,000.00
1902-S	1,780.00	1,800.00
1903	1,780.00	1,800.00
1903-S	1,780.00	1,800.00
1904	1,780.00	1,800.00
1904-S	1,780.00	1,800.00
1905	1,785.00	1,820.00
1905-S	1,780.00	1,800.00
1906	1,785.00	1,800.00
1906-D	1,780.00	1,800.00
1906-S	1,780.00	1,800.00
1907	1,780.00	1,800.00
1907-D	1,780.00	1,800.00
1907-S	1,780.00	1,800.00

SAINT-GAUDENS GOLD $20

Sculptor Augustus Saint-Gaudens designed President Theodore Roosevelt's inaugural medal. Roosevelt liked the result so much that he commissioned the sculptor to improve the design of U.S. coinage. The results included a striking new design for the gold $20 coin in 1907, considered by many to be the most beautiful coin in U.S. history. Roosevelt wanted the new $20 coin to emulate the high-relief style of ancient Greek coins. Although an artistic triumph, the high relief of the first 1907 Saint-Gaudens gold $20 coins caused production problems and would not allow the coins to stack properly. Thus, the relief was lowered, and Arabic numerals were used in the date instead of Roman numerals.

Congressional acts of March 3, 1865, and Feb. 12, 1873, allowed the motto "In God We Trust" to be placed on U.S. coins but did not mandate it. According to author Don Taxay, Roosevelt considered it sacrilege to use a religious motto on coinage. When the new 1907 gold $10 and $20 coins appeared without the motto, Congress passed legislation on May 18, 1908, mandating its use on all coins on which it had previously appeared.

The Gold Reserve Act of Jan. 30, 1934, discontinued the production of all U.S. gold coinage. Most of the 1933 gold $20 coins produced were still in government vaults at the time and were melted, but a few examples illicitly found their way into private hands. The U.S. government allowed one of them to be sold in 2002, but any others that turn up are still subject to confiscation.

Saint-Gaudens gold $20, date in Roman numerals.

Saint-Gaudens, Date in Roman Numerals	VF	XF
MCMVII (1907) wire rim	7,650.00	8,750.00
MCMVII (1907) flat rim	7,900.00	9,250.00

1907 Saint-Gaudens gold $20, date in Arabic numerals.

Saint-Gaudens, Date in Arabic Numerals	VF	XF
1907	1,795.00	1,830.00
1908	1,785.00	1,820.00
1908-D	1,795.00	1,830.00

1908 Saint-Gaudens gold $20,
motto below eagle.

Saint-Gaudens, Motto Below Eagle	VF	XF
1908	1,790.00	1,825.00
1908-D	1,795.00	1,830.00
1908-S	2,450.00	3,150.00
1909	1,800.00	1,850.00
1909-D	1,835.00	1,870.00
1909-S	1,795.00	1,830.00
1910	1,790.00	1,825.00
1910-D	1,790.00	1,825.00
1910-S	1,795.00	1,830.00
1911	1,795.00	1,830.00
1911-D	1,790.00	1,825.00
1911-S	1,790.00	1,825.00
1912	1,795.00	1,830.00
1913	1,795.00	1,830.00
1913-D	1,790.00	1,825.00
1913-S	1,845.00	1,880.00
1914	1,800.00	1,840.00
1914-D	1,790.00	1,825.00
1914-S	1,790.00	1,825.00
1915	1,795.00	1,830.00
1915-S	1,790.00	1,825.00
1916-S	1,795.00	1,830.00
1920	1,785.00	1,820.00
1920-S	14,500.00	18,500.00
1921	35,000.00	43,500.00
1922	1,785.00	1,820.00
1922-S	1,900.00	2,000.00
1923	1,785.00	1,820.00
1923-D	1,795.00	1,830.00
1924	1,785.00	1,820.00
1924-D	2,010.00	2,040.00
1924-S	1,665.00	1,750.00
1925	1,785.00	1,820.00
1925-D	1,950.00	2,100.00
1925-S	1,900.00	2,850.00
1926	1,785.00	1,820.00

Saint-Gaudens, Motto Below Eagle	VF	XF
1926-D	10,000.00	15,500.00
1926-S	1,490.00	1,550.00
1927	1,785.00	1,820.00
1927-D	155,000.00	200,000.00
1927-S	6,850.00	8,850.00
1928	1,785.00	1,820.00
1929	10,000.00	13,500.00
1930-S	35,000.00	41,000.00
1931	10,500.00	13,500.00
1931-D	8,850.00	11,500.00
1932	12,500.00	14,500.00
1933, 13 known	—	—

2009 ULTRAHIGH RELIEF

The 2009 ultrahigh-relief gold $20 revived the classic Saint-Gaudens gold $20 design for one year only in a special issue sold by the U.S. Mint at a premium directly to collectors.

2009 Ultrahigh Relief	PF-65
2009	2,850.00

2009 Saint-Gaudens gold $20, ultrahigh relief.

MODERN COMMEMORATIVES

After a 28-year break, the U.S. Mint resumed issuing commemorative coins when it released a half dollar marking the 250th anniversary of George Washington's birth in 1982. The congressionally authorized coin was a hit. The Mint sold more than 2.2 million uncirculated versions and almost 4.9 million proof versions.

A myriad of issues have followed in clad, silver, and gold compositions, and in denominations ranging from a half dollar to $10.

Commemorative coins honor events, people, or other things, and are individually authorized by law. They are official U.S. government issues and legal tender, but they are not intended to circulate. Instead, the U.S. Mint sells the coins directly to collectors at a premium above face value. Laws authorizing commemorative coins usually mandate that a certain amount of the purchase price benefit a group or event related to the coin's theme.

By the 1990s, commemorative coins had become an easy mark for senators and U.S. representatives looking to do a favor for a constituency or a favor for a fellow lawmaker by offering their vote for a commemorative coin program. The year 1994 alone brought five commemorative coin programs, and the proliferation caused sales to plummet.

In response, Congress passed the Commemorative Coin Reform Act of 1996. Among other provisions, it limits the number of commemorative themes to two per year.

Current-year commemoratives can be purchased directly from the U.S. Mint (www.usmint.gov). Issues from previous years can be purchased on the secondary market (shows, shops, and advertisements in coin-collecting magazines) for the going market rate, as reflected in the values that follow.

2008-S Bald Eagle clad half dollar.

2013 Five-Star Generals clad half dollar.

Clad Half Dollars	MS-65	PF-65
1986 Statue of Liberty Centennial	3.25	3.50
1989 Bicentennial of the Congress	7.50	7.50
1991 Mount Rushmore Golden Anniversary	17.50	16.00
1991-1995 World War II 50th Anniversary	17.00	16.50
1992 Olympics	8.50	8.50
1992 500th Anniversary of Columbus Discovery	11.50	8.75
1994 World Cup	8.25	8.00
1995 Atlanta Olympics, baseball design	19.50	17.50
1995 Atlanta Olympics, basketball design	18.00	17.00
1995 Civil War	36.50	33.50
1996 Atlanta Olympics, soccer design	130.00	90.00
1996 Atlanta Olympics, swimming design	140.00	30.00
2001 U.S. Capitol	14.50	15.50
2003 First Flight Centennial	15.00	17.00
2008 Bald Eagle	12.50	14.00
2011 U.S. Army	70.00	35.00
2013 Five-Star Generals	50.00	60.00
2015 Baseball Hall of Fame	50.00	60.00

1982 George Washington 250th Anniversary
of Birth silver half dollar.

Silver Half Dollars	MS-65	PF-65
1982 George Washington 250th Anniversary of Birth	13.75	13.75
1993 James Madison, Bill of Rights	19.00	19.00
Silver Dollars	**MS-65**	**PF-65**
1983 Los Angeles XXIII Olympiad	35.00	37.00
1984 Los Angeles XXIII Olympiad	35.00	37.00
1986 Statue of Liberty Centennial	35.00	37.00
1987 U.S. Constitution 200th Anniversary	35.00	37.00
1988 Olympiad	35.00	37.00
1989 Bicentennial of the Congress	35.00	37.00
1990 Eisenhower Centennial	35.00	37.00
1991 38th Anniversary Korean War	38.00	37.00
1991 Mount Rushmore Golden Anniversary	40.00	43.00
1991 USO 50th Anniversary	38.00	39.00
1991-1995 World War II 50th Anniversary	37.00	40.00
1992 Olympics	38.00	39.00
1992 Columbus Quincentenary	40.00	38.00
1992 The White House 1792-1992	38.00	39.00
1993 James Madison	38.00	39.00
1993 Thomas Jefferson 1743-1993	37.00	40.00
1994 World Cup	39.00	37.00
1994 National Prisoner of War Museum	84.00	40.00
1994 Bicentennial of United States Capitol	39.00	40.00
1994 Vietnam Veterans Memorial	80.00	63.00
1994 Women in Military Service Memorial	39.00	39.00
1995 Atlanta Olympics, cycling design	135.00	45.00
1995 Atlanta Olympics, gymnastics design	55.00	37.00
1995 Atlanta Olympics, track and field design	88.00	39.00
1995 Atlanta Olympics, Paralympics design	67.00	45.00
1995 Civil War	65.00	55.00
1995 Special Olympics World Games	40.00	42.00

1994-P Women in Military Service Memorial silver dollar.

Silver Dollars	MS-65	PF-65
1996 Atlanta Olympics, high-jump design	310.00	43.00
1996 Atlanta Olympics, rowing design	290.00	62.00
1996 Atlanta Olympics, tennis design	245.00	83.00
1996 Atlanta Olympics, Paralympics design	300.00	70.00
1996 National Community Service	170.00	50.00
1996 Smithsonian Institution 1846-1996	120.00	50.00
1997 Jackie Robinson 50th Anniversary	70.00	90.00
1997 National Law Enforcement Officers Memorial	80.00	135.00
1997 United States Botanic Garden 1820-1995	42.00	42.00
1998 Black Revolutionary War Patriots	145.00	90.00
1998 Robert F. Kennedy	45.00	45.00
1999 Dolley Madison	38.00	38.00
1999 Yellowstone National Park	44.00	40.00
2000 Leif Ericson	70.00	60.00
2000 Library of Congress 1800-2000	40.00	38.00
2001 American Buffalo	165.00	170.00
2001 U.S. Capitol	40.00	40.00
2002 XIX Olympic Winter Games	40.00	38.00
2002 West Point Bicentennial	38.00	40.00
2003 First Flight Centennial	40.00	45.00
2004 Lewis and Clark Bicentennial	40.00	45.00
2004 125th Anniversary of the Light Bulb	40.00	42.00
2005 Chief Justice John Marshall	37.00	35.00
2005 Marines 1775-2005	48.00	52.00
2006 Benjamin Franklin Tercentenary, kite-flying design	40.00	45.00
2006 Benjamin Franklin Tercentenary, portrait design	40.00	50.00
2006 San Francisco Old Mint	40.00	40.00
2007 Desegregation in Education	40.00	43.00
2007 Founding of Jamestown 1607-2007	40.00	38.00

2013 Girl Scouts of America Centennial silver dollar.

Silver Dollars	MS-65	PF-65
2008 Bald Eagle	44.00	38.00
2009 Abraham Lincoln	55.00	55.00
2009 Louis Braille 1809-2009	38.00	38.00
2010 Disabled Veterans	40.00	42.00
2010 Boy Scouts of America 1910-2010	38.00	42.00
2011 Medal of Honor, 1861-2011	46.00	43.00
2011 U.S. Army	45.00	43.00
2012 Star Spangled Banner Bicentennial	50.00	60.00
2012 U.S. Infantry	50.00	60.00
2013 Five-Star Generals	50.00	60.00
2013 Girl Scouts of America Centennial	50.00	60.00
2014 1964 Civil Rights Act	50.00	60.00
2015 Baseball Hall of Fame	50.00	60.00
2015 U.S. Marshal Service 225th anniversary	—	—
2017 Lions Clubs International Centennial	—	—

PROOF SETS

Proof coins are struck from specially selected, highly polished planchets and dies. They usually receive multiple strikes from the coining press at increased pressure. The results are coins with mirrorlike surfaces and, in recent years, a cameo effect on their raised design surfaces. The coins are then carefully handled; placed in sealed, inert holders; and sold to collectors by the U.S. Mint in sets.

Proof coins originated centuries ago when specially

produced pieces were prepared as examples of the ideal coin, often for reference or royal approval. U.S. proof coins date back to the early 1800s, but they were not widely available. They were struck for VIPs and coin collectors and dealers with connections at the U.S. Mint. In 1936, the Mint began selling proof sets to the general public.

Traditionally, the sets contain one proof example of each coin struck for circulation that year, but with the proliferation of commemorative coins and other special issues, such as the 50 State Quarters, the Mint has offered multiple proof sets in a single year.

The 50 State Quarters, 2009 District of Columbia and U.S. Territories quarters, and America the Beautiful Quarters are included in regular proof sets for their respective years but were also offered in separate five-piece sets containing only the quarters.

Proof sets contain only one example of each coin (no multiple mint marks). Most proof coins are struck at the San Francisco Mint and have an "S" mint mark.

For 1983, some proof sets contain dimes with no "S" mint mark, which was a production error. In 1990, some proof sets contain one-cent coins with no "S" mint mark, also the result of a production error.

Current-year sets can be purchased directly from the U.S. Mint (www.usmint.gov). Sets from previous years can be purchased on the secondary market at the going price. Values listed below are for officially issued U.S. Mint proof sets in their original packaging.

Date	Value
1936	7,500.00
1937	4,350.00
1938	1,900.00
1939	1,800.00
1940	1,385.00
1941	1,450.00
1942, 6 coins	1,475.00

Date	Value
1942, 5 coins	1,250.00
1950	540.00
1951	565.00
1952	225.00
1953	210.00
1954	110.00
1955 box	90.00
1955 flat pack	120.00
1956	53.00
1957	30.00
1958	35.00
1959	30.00
1960, large date	30.00
1960, small date	35.00
1961	25.00
1962	25.00
1963	25.00
1964	25.00
1968-S	7.75
1968-S, no-mint-mark dime	16,500.00
1969-S	7.25
1970-S, large date	9.00
1970-S, small date	75.00
1970-S, no-mint-mark dime	855.00
1971-S	5.00
1971-S, no-mint-mark nickel	5.00
1972-S	5.50
1973-S	8.25
1974-S	9.00
1975-S	7.75
1975-S, no-mint-mark dime	7.75
1976-S, 3 coins	25.00
1976-S	6.60
1977-S	7.00
1978-S	6.00
1979-S, type 1	6.00
1979-S, type 2	65.00
1980-S	3.75
1981-S, type 1	5.50
1981-S, type 2	285.00
1982-S	3.50

Date	Value
1983-S	3.50
1983-S, no-mint-mark dime	600.00
1983-S, Prestige Set	60.00
1984-S	4.75
1984-S, Prestige Set	35.00
1985-S	3.75
1986-S	5.00
1986-S, Prestige Set	35.00
1987-S	4.50
1987-S, Prestige Set	35.00
1988-S	6.00
1988-S, Prestige Set	35.00
1989-S	4.00
1989-S, Prestige Set	40.00
1990-S	4.50
1990-S, no-mint-mark cent	5,100.00
1990-S, Prestige Set	35.00
1990-S, Prestige Set no-mint-mark cent	5,100.00
1991-S	4.75
1991-S, Prestige Set	40.00
1992-S	4.50
1992-S, Prestige Set	45.00
1992-S, silver	21.00
1992-S, silver Premier Set	25.00
1993-S	4.50
1993-S, Prestige Set	52.00
1993-S, silver	32.50
1993-S, silver Premier Set	35.00
1994-S	5.25
1994-S, Prestige Set	45.00
1994-S, silver	25.00
1994-S, silver Premier Set	30.00
1995-S	10.00
1995-S, Prestige Set	95.00
1995-S, silver	45.00
1995-S, silver Premier Set	60.00
1996-S	7.50
1996-S, Prestige Set	270.00
1996-S, silver	25.00
1996-S, silver Premier Set	35.00
1997-S	11.25

Date	Value
1997-S, Prestige Set	70.00
1997-S, silver	35.00
1997-S, silver Premier Set	40.00
1998-S	8.75
1998-S, silver	25.00
1998-S, silver Premier Set	30.00
1999-S	10.00
1999-S, 5-piece quarters set	6.00
1999-S, silver	120.00
2000-S	5.75
2000-S, 5-piece quarters set	3.50
2000-S, silver	45.00
2001-S	12.75
2001-S, 5-piece quarters set	7.50
2001-S, silver	50.00
2002-S	7.75
2002-S, 5-piece quarters set	4.50
2002-S, silver	50.00
2003-S	8.00
2003-S, 5-piece quarters set	3.50
2003-S, silver	50.00
2004-S	9.00
2004-S, 5-piece quarters set	4.50
2004-S, silver	45.00
2004-S, silver 5-piece quarters set	30.00
2005-S	6.00
2005,-S 5-piece quarters set	3.25
2005-S, silver	45.00
2005-S, silver 5-piece quarters set	30.00
2006-S	9.00
2006-S, 5-piece quarters set	4.50
2006-S silver	45.00
2006-S, silver 5-piece quarters set	30.00
2007-S	13.75
2007-S, 5-piece quarters set	4.50
2007-S, silver	55.00
2007-S, silver 5-piece quarters set	30.00
2007-S, 4-piece Presidential Dollars set	6.00
2008-S	80.00
2008-S, 5-piece quarters set	30.00
2008-S, 4-piece Presidential Dollars set	10.00

Date	Value
2008-S, silver	60.00
2008-S, silver 5-piece quarters set	30.00
2009-S	20.00
2009-S, 4-piece Lincoln Bicentennial Cents set	15.00
2009-S, 6-piece quarters set	10.00
2009-S, 4-piece Presidential Dollars set	8.25
2009-S, silver	60.00
2009-S, 6-piece silver quarters set	35.00
2010-S	45.00
2010-S ,5-piece quarters set	25.00
2010-S, 4-piece Presidential Dollars set	15.00
2010-S, silver	50.00
2010-S, 5-piece silver quarters set	30.00
2011-S	35.00
2011-S, 5-piece quarters set	15.00
2011-S, 4-piece Presidential Dollars set	20.00
2011-S, silver	70.00
2011-S, 5-piece silver quarters set	30.00
2012-S	40.00
2012-S, 5-piece quarters set	18.00
2012-S, 4-piece Presidential Dollars set	20.00
2012-S, silver	65.00
2012-S, 5-piece silver quarters set	40.00

$100 and $10 Star Note

Paper Money introduction

The first paper money to circulate in the United States was issued during the Colonial era. British mercantile policies resulted in a chronic shortage of precious-metal coinage in the Colonies, and the paper issues helped fill the void.

During the Revolutionary War, the states and Continental Congress continued to issue paper money, but its backing in hard currency was spotty at best. Inflation ensued, and the notes' value plummeted. Some were called "shinplasters" because early Americans put them in their boots to help keep their feet warm. The saying "not worth a Continental" had its roots in the devaluation of Continental currency.

Designs on state notes varied, but most featured inscriptions within elaborate borders. Coats of arms and crowns were also common. During the mid-1770s, designs became more elaborate; farm scenes and buildings were popular design subjects. Most Continental currency bore intricate circular seals of allegories.

To deter counterfeiting, leaves were used in the printing process. The fine detail of a leaf on a note was difficult for counterfeiters to duplicate. Each note was hand signed, sometimes by important figures in early American history. The significance of a note's signatures can enhance its value.

Because of the devaluation of paper money during the Colonial and Continental Congress eras, the Constitution specified that "no state shall ... make anything but gold and silver coin a tender in payment of debts." This provision, however, still allowed banks and other private institutions to issue paper money, which circulated solely on the people's trust in the issuing entity. Sound banks kept enough hard-money reserves to redeem their notes on demand; less scrupulous banks didn't.

Known as "obsolete notes" or "broken bank notes" today, these private issues were produced in especially large numbers in the 1830s and 1850s. They became obsolete in the 1860s when many of the issuing banks went under while others redeemed their outstanding notes and did not issue more. The notes are valued by collectors today because many of them feature artistic vignettes of local industries, such as shipping or cotton, or patriotic themes provided by the printer. Some show their value in coins – two half dollars and a quarter to represent $1.25, for example. Most obsolete notes are one-sided.

During the Civil War, the public hoarded gold, silver, and even copper coins. In response to the resulting coin shortage, postage stamps were used for small change in everyday transactions. The stamps were placed in small envelopes printed with a value, but the envelopes deteriorated quickly and the stamps soon became a sticky mess.

The solution was to issue small, rectangular-shaped "postage currency" in 1862. Depictions of postage stamps on the currency indicated their value; a 50-cent note depicted 50 cents in postage stamps, for example. They could not be used as postage on letters or packages (they had no adhesive), but they could be redeemed at any post office for the indicated amount of postage.

In 1863, fractional currency replaced the postage currency. It was similar in size to the postage currency but did not contain any reference to postage stamps. Fractional notes were issued through 1876, by which time coinage production had caught up with demand and the hoarding of the Civil War era had ended. Fractional currency is common in the collectibles market today. Many issues can be purchased for $20 to $100, depending on the individual note and its condition.

Demand notes are considered the first regular paper money issued by the U.S. government and lead off the listings that follow.

The paper-money issues in the following listings are identified first by type, using the names commonly used by collectors. They are further identified by denomination and series date, which is not necessarily the date in which the piece was issued. "Series" indicates the year of the act authorizing the series or the year production of the series began. Further means of identifying notes include their design, seal color, issuing bank, signers, and size. Through 1928, U.S. paper-money issues were about 7 1/2 inches by 3 1/8 inches and are commonly called "large-size notes" today. Beginning with Series 1928 (released in 1929), U.S. paper-money issues were reduced to 6 1/8 inches by 2 5/8 inches and are commonly called "small-size notes."

GRADING U.S. PAPER MONEY

CRISP UNCIRCULATED (CU) describes a perfectly preserved note that never has been mishandled by the issuing authority, a bank teller, the public, or a collector. The paper is clean and firm without discoloration. Corners are sharp and square, with no evidence of rounding. (Rounded corners often indicate a cleaned or "doctored" note.) The note will have its original, natural sheen.

ABOUT UNCIRCULATED (AU) describes a virtually perfect note that shows signs of some minor handling. It may show evidence of bank-counting folds at a corner or one light fold through the center but not both. An AU note cannot be creased (a crease is defined as a hard fold that has usually broken the note's surface). The paper is clean and bright with original sheen. Corners are not rounded.

EXTREMELY FINE (XF) describes an attractive note with signs of light handling. It may have a maximum of three light folds or one strong crease. The paper is clean and bright with original sheen. Corners may show only the slightest evidence of rounding. There may also be the slightest signs of wear where a fold meets the edge.

VERY FINE (VF) describes an attractive note with more evidence of handling and wear. Vertical and horizontal folds may be present. The paper may have minimal dirt or color smudging. The paper itself is still relatively crisp and not floppy. There should be no tears in the border area, although the edges will show slight wear. Corners will also show wear but not full rounding.

FINE (F) describes a note that has seen considerable circulation. Many folds, creases, and wrinkling will be present. The paper is not excessively dirty but may have some softness. Edges may show signs of much handling with minor tears in the border area. Tears may not extend into the design. There should be no center hole from excessive folding. Colors should be clear, but they may not be very bright. A staple hole or two is not considered unusual wear on a note grading fine. The note's overall appearance is still desirable.

VERY GOOD (VG) describes a well-used but still intact note. Corners may have much wear and rounding. There may be tiny nicks, tears extending into the design, some discoloration and staining, and possibly a small center hole from excessive folding. Staple and pin holes are usually present, and the paper itself is quite limp.

GOOD (G) describes a well-worn and heavily used note. Normal damage from prolonged circulation may include strong multiple folds and creases, stains, staple or pin holes or both, dirt, discoloration, edge tears, a center hole, rounded corners, and an overall unattractive appearance. No large pieces of the note may be missing.

FAIR (F) describes a totally limp, dirty, and well-used note. Large pieces may be torn off or missing.

POOR (P) describes a note with severe damage from wear, staining, missing pieces, graffiti, and larger holes. Tape may be holding pieces of the note together. Rough edges may have been trimmed off.

In addition, follow these rules for handling collectible paper money:

FOLDING always damages a note. Never fold a piece of collectible paper money.

CLEANING, WASHING, AND PRESSING paper money is also harmful and reduces a note's grade and subsequent value. A washed or pressed note will probably lose its original sheen, and its surface may become lifeless and dull. A pressed note may still show evidence of folds and creases under a good light, and washed notes may have white streaks where the folds or creases were.

PAPER MONEY PRICING

DEMAND NOTES

The demand notes of 1861 were the first paper money issued by the U.S. government, as an emergency measure during the Civil War. At first, they were not officially legal tender, so merchants and other private individuals were not obligated to accept them in payment for goods and services. But they were "receivable in payment for all public dues," so they could be used to pay taxes, for example. Later, a law was passed requiring their acceptance in private transactions also. The name "demand notes" comes from the statement on their face: "The United States promises to pay to the bearer on demand."

There were limits, however, on how demand notes could be redeemed. The notes were issued at five cities and could be redeemed by the assistant treasurers only in the individual note's specific city of issue.

Designs were uniform among issues from all cities. The $5 note shows at left the statue of Columbia from the U.S. Capitol and at right a portrait of Alexander Hamilton. The $10 shows Abraham Lincoln (then in office) at left, an eagle in the center, and an allegorical figure of art at right. The $20 depicts Liberty holding a sword and shield. The nickname "greenback" for paper

money began with these notes, which have a distinctive green back. The privately issued obsolete notes, which preceded demand notes, had blank backs.

There are two major varieties of demand notes. Originally clerks were to hand sign the notes as "for the" Treasury register and "for the" U.S. treasurer. To save clerks the time required to write "for the" millions of times, the words were printed on later notes instead of handwritten. The earlier variety, with "for the" handwritten, are worth more than the prices listed here.

High-grade notes in this series are rare.

	F	VF
$5 Boston	3,200.00	5,500.00
$5 Cincinnati, rare	—	—
$5 New York	3,400.00	4,400.00
$5 Philadelphia	3,300.00	4,500.00
$5 St. Louis	18,000.00	38,000.00
$10 Boston	18,000.00	22,000.00
$10 Cincinnati	16,000.00	20,000.00
$10 New York	10,000.00	20,000.00
$10 Philadelphia	5,000.00	15,000.00
$10 St. Louis	12,000.00	75,000.00
$20 Boston	—	75,000.00
$20 Cincinnati	2,500.00	—
$20 New York	—	80,500.00
$20 Philadelphia	—	100,000.00

TREASURY NOTES

Treasury notes are also called "coin notes" because the Treasury secretary was required to redeem them in his choice of gold or silver coin, although the notes were backed by silver bullion rather than coins.

Treasury notes were issued only in 1890 and 1891. Both years have the same face designs, generally of military heroes. The original reverse designs featured the values spelled out in large letters. For 1891, they were redesigned to allow more blank space. The ornamentation of the two 0s in 100 on the reverse of the $100 notes looks like the pattern on the skin of a watermelon. Hence, they are known in the collecting community as "watermelon notes."

	F	XF
$1 1890 Edwin M. Stanton	400.00	2,000.00
$1 1891 Edwin M. Stanton	210.00	450.00
$2 1890 Gen. James D. McPherson	650.00	4,000.00
$2 1891 Gen. James D. McPherson	460.00	1,400.00
$5 1890 Gen. George H. Thomas	550.00	5,800.00
$5 1891 Gen. George H. Thomas	550.00	1,400.00
$10 1890 Gen. Philip H. Sheridan	1,400.00	5,500.00
$10 1891 Gen. Philip H. Sheridan	1,000.00	2,500.00
$20 1890 John Marshall	3,125.00	10,000.00
$20 1891 John Marshall	8,500.00	17,500.00
$50 1891 William H. Seward	—	125,000.00
$100 1890 Adm. David G. Farragut	—	185,000.00
$100 1891 Adm. David G. Farragut	63,250.00	150,000.00
$1,000 1890 Gen. George Meade	—	1,095,000.00
$1,000 1891 Gen. George Meade, rare	—	—

NATIONAL BANK NOTES

National bank notes were a collaboration between private, nationally charted banks and the U.S. government. Individual banks could invest in U.S. bonds and, in return, receive paper money with a face value equal to their investment. The federal government designed and printed the notes. Designs were the same for each bank, but notes were imprinted with the name and charter number of the national bank receiving them. Some early notes also bear the coat of arms of the issuing bank's state.

National bank notes, titled "National Currency" on their faces, were legal tender anywhere in the United States and could be redeemed at the issuing bank or the U.S. Treasury. Notes redeemed at the Treasury were charged against the issuing bank's bond account. More than 1,300 national banks issued notes.

There were three periods during which banks could apply for a 20-year nationally issued charter: (1) 1863-1882, (2) 1882-1902, and (3) 1902-1922. Banks could issue notes under the first charter period until 1902, under the second charter period until 1922, and under the third charter period until 1929. Notes issued under each charter period have different designs.

Like all other U.S. paper money, national bank notes were reduced in size in 1929. Type 1 notes (1929-1933) list the charter number on the face twice. Type 2 notes (1933-1935) list it four times.

National bank notes were discontinued in May 1935 when the Treasury recalled many of the bonds in which the national banks had invested.

Nationals have been among the most sought-after notes in a generally active U.S. paper-money market. Not all nationals of a given type have the same value; notes of certain states and cities are more popularly collected than others. Also, some banks ordered only small quantities of notes. The values listed below are for the most common and least expensive banks issuing that type of note. Large-size nationals from Alaska, Arizona, Hawaii, Idaho, Indian Territory, Mississippi, Nevada, New Mexico, Puerto Rico, and South Dakota are worth more. The same is true for small-size nationals from Alaska, Arizona, Hawaii, Idaho, Montana, Nevada, and Wyoming.

First Charter (1863-1875)	VG	VF
$1 Allegory of Concord, no date, original series	600.00	1,050.00
$1 Allegory of Concord, 1875	600.00	1,050.00
$2 Sir Walter Raleigh, "lazy 2," no date, original series	3,600.00	5,750.00
$2 Sir Walter Raleigh, 1875	1,500.00	4,000.00
$5 Columbus sighting land, no date, original series	725.00	1,650.00
$5 Columbus sighting land, 1875	725.00	1,650.00
$10 Franklin flying kite, no date, original series	1,000.00	2,000.00
$10 Franklin flying kite, 1875	1,000.00	2,000.00
$20 Battle of Lexington, no date, original series	2,500.00	4,000.00
$20 Battle of Lexington, 1875	1,600.00	3,250.00
$50 Washington crossing the Delaware, no date, original series	15,000.00	25,000.00
$50 Washington crossing the Delaware, 1875	15,000.00	25,000.00
$100 Battle of Lake Erie, no date, original series	17,000.00	35,000.00

First Charter (1863-1875)	VG	VF
$100 Battle of Lake Erie, 1875	17,000.00	35,000.00
$500 Arrival of the Sirius, no date, original series rare	—	—
$500 Arrival of the Sirius, 1875 rare	—	—
$1,000 Scott entering Mexico City, no date, original series rare	—	—
$1,000 Scott entering Mexico City, 1875 1 known	—	—

Second Charter, Series of 1882 "Brown Backs" with Charter Number On Back	VG	VF
$5 James Garfield	450.00	650.00
$10 Franklin flying kite	500.00	750.00
$20 Battle of Lexington	575.00	850.00
$50 Washington crossing Delaware	4,500.00	5,175.00
$100 Battle of Lake Erie	5,500.00	10,350.00

Second Charter, Series of 1882 "Date Backs," large "1882*1908" on back	VG	VF
$5 James Garfield	425.00	575.00
$10 Franklin flying kite	400.00	800.00
$20 Battle of Lexington	550.00	800.00
$50 Washington Crossing Delaware	5,500.00	6,500.00
$100 Battle of Lake Erie	7,500.00	8,250.00

Second Charter, Series of 1882,"Value Backs," Value Spelled Out on Back	VG	VF
$5 James Garfield	500.00	1,025.00
$10 Franklin flying kite	450.00	800.00
$20 Battle of Lexington	750.00	1,300.00
$50 Washington crossing Delaware, rare	—	—
$100 Battle of Lake Erie, rare	—	—

Third Charter, Series of 1902, Red Treasury Seal on Face	VG	VF
$5 Benjamin Harrison	400.00	550.00
$10 William McKinley	350.00	850.00
$20 Hugh McCulloch	450.00	625.00
$50 John Sherman	5,750.00	6,000.00
$100 John Knox	7,500.00	11,000.00

Third Charter, Series of 1902, Blue Treasury Seal, 1902-1908 on Back	VG	VF
$5 Benjamin Harrison	150.00	350.00
$10 William McKinley	150.00	350.00
$20 Hugh McCulloch	175.00	325.00
$50 John Sherman	700.00	825.00
$100 John Knox	850.00	1,250.00

Third Charter, Series of 1902, Blue Treasury Seal, "Plain Backs," Without Dates	VG	VF
$5 Benjamin Harrison	100.00	200.00
$10 William McKinley	125.00	225.00
$20 Hugh McCulloch	150.00	300.00
$50 John Sherman	700.00	825.00
$100 John Knox	800.00	1,250.00
$100 Type 1	560.00	675.00

Third Charter, Series of 1929, Brown Treasury Seal, Small Size	VG	VF
$5 Type 1	50.00	100.00
$5 Type 2	60.00	100.00
$10 Type 1	60.00	90.00
$10 Type 2	75.00	175.00
$20 Type 1	60.00	85.00
$20 Type 2	70.00	125.00
$50 Type 1	80.00	125.00
$50 Type 2	200.00	400.00
$100 Type 1	175.00	250.00
$100 Type 2	225.00	350.00

NATIONAL GOLD BANK NOTES

National gold bank notes were similar to national bank notes but were redeemable specifically in gold coin. They were issued by nationally chartered banks that were authorized by the Treasury to issue notes redeemable in gold.

They were issued from 1870 to 1875 to relieve California banks from handling mass quantities of gold coin. All but one of the banks authorized to issue the notes were located in California.

National gold bank notes were printed on golden-yellow paper and depict an assortment of U.S. gold coins on their reverse designs. Fine engraving resulted in high-quality images.

Because other types of notes were not popular in California, national gold bank notes saw heavy use and are scarce today in collectible condition.

	G	F
$5 Columbus sighting land	1,750.00	7,500.00
$10 Franklin flying kite	4,000.00	20,000.00
$20 Battle of Lexington	8,000.00	30,000.00
$50 Washington Crossing the Delaware, rare	—	—
$100 Battle of Lake Erie	100,000	258,000

UNITED STATES NOTES

Most of these notes are titled "United States Note" at the top or bottom of their faces, but some earlier ones are titled "Treasury Note." The first United States notes omit both, but all were authorized under the same legislation. They were issued for more than a century (1862-1966) and thus are the longest-running type of U.S. paper money.

The series contains many classic designs. The most popular is the $10 with a bison on its face.

Like other currency, United States notes were reduced in size with Series 1928, printed in 1929. Small-size United States notes occasionally are still found in circulation today and are distinguished by a red Treasury seal. They generally are not collectible in worn condition.

This series includes popular "star notes," which have part of the serial number replaced by a star. They were printed to replace notes accidentally destroyed in manufacturing. These were introduced on $20 notes in 1880 and eventually descended to $1 notes by 1917. They usually are worth more than regularly numbered notes.

Large Size	F	XF
$1 1862 Salmon P. Chase, red seal	325.00	850.00
$1 1869 George Washington	400.00	2,200.00
$1 1874 George Washington	200.00	835.00

Large Size	F	XF
$1 1875 George Washington	200.00	600.00
$1 1878 George Washington	275.00	650.00
$1 1880 George Washington	200.00	400.00
$1 1917 George Washington	60.00	115.00
$1 1923 George Washington	125.00	275.00
$1 1869 George Washington	400.00	2,200.00
$2 1869 Jefferson, Capitol	700.00	3,250.00
$2 1874 Jefferson, Capitol	460.00	1,200.00
$2 1875 Jefferson, Capitol	480.00	1,200.00
$2 1878 Jefferson, Capitol	380.00	800.00
$2 1880 Jefferson, Capitol	275.00	600.00
$5 1862 Statue of Columbia, Alexander Hamilton	575.00	1,750.00
$5 1863 same, different obligation on back 450	1,100.00	835.00
$5 1869 Andrew Jackson, pioneer family 600	1,800.00	3,250.00
$5 1875 same, red seal 250	700.00	1,200.00
$5 1880 same, brown seal 440	600.00	1,200.00
$10 1862 Lincoln, allegory of art 1,000	2,250.00	3,250.00
$10 1863 same, different obligation on back	1,450.00	3,000.00
$10 1869 Daniel Webster, Pocahontas	1,300.00	1,800.00
$10 1875 same, different obligation on back	1,000.00	3,000.00
$10 1878 same	1,150.00	2,250.00
$10 1880 same, brown seal	500.00	1,300.00
$10 1880 same, large red seal	400.00	1,000.00
$10 1880 same, small red seal	375.00	1,250.00
$10 1901 bison	600.00	2,000.00
$10 1923 Andrew Jackson	1,750.00	5,250.00
$20 1862 Liberty with sword and shield	2,300.00	6,750.00
$20 1863 same, different obligation on back	2,000.00	4,000.00
$20 1869 Alexander Hamilton, Victory	2,900.00	10,000.00
$20 1875 same, no inscription at center on back	1,500.00	2,750.00
$20 1878 same 900	1,800.00	2,250.00
$20 1880 same, brown seal	750.00	2,500.00
$20 1880 same, large red seal	400.00	1,750.00
$20 1880 same, small red seal	350.00	1,250.00
$50 1862 Alexander Hamilton	32,500.00	43,125.00
$50 1863 same, different obligation on back	12,500.00	300,000.00

Large Size	F	XF
$50 1869 Peace, Henry Clay	21,500.00	50,000.00
$50 1874 Benjamin Franklin, Columbia	10,000.00	15,000.00
$50 1875 same, rare	1,000.00	3,000.00
$50 1878 same	5,000.00	20,000.00
$50 1880 same, brown seal	5,000.00	30,000.00
$50 1880 same, large red seal	6,000.00	14,000.00
$50 1880 same, small red seal	2,000.00	6,325.00
$100 1862 eagle	30,000.00	50,000.00
$100 1863 same, different obligation on back, rare	—	—
$100 1869 Lincoln, allegory of Architecture	17,500.00	18,400.00
$100 1875 same	15,000.00	40,000.00
$100 1878 same	15,000.00	30,000.00
$100 1880 same, inscription at left on back, brown seal	9,000.00	30,000.00
$100 1880 same, large red seal	14,000.00	35,000.00
$100 1880 same, small red seal	6,000.00	17,500.00
$500 1862 Albert Gallatin, rare	—	—
$500 1863 same, different obligation on back, rare	—	—
$500 1869 John Quincy Adams, rare	—	—
$500 1874 Gen. Joseph Mansfield, rare	—	—
$500 1875 same, rare	—	—
$500 1878 same, rare	—	—
$500 1880 Gen. Joseph Mansfield, brown seal, rare	—	—
$500 1880 same, large red seal, rare	—	—
$500 1880 same, small red seal, rare	—	—
$1,000 1862 Robert Morris, none known	—	—
$1,000 1863 same, different obligation on back, rare	—	—
$1,000 1869 Columbus, DeWitt Clinton, rare	—	—
$1,000 1878 same, rare	—	—
$1,000 1880 same, inscription at left, brown seal rare	—	—
$1,000 1880 same, large red seal, rare	—	—
$1,000 1880 same, small red seal, rare	—	—

SMALL-SIZE U.S. NOTES, RED SEAL

Denom.	Series	Front	Back
$1	1928	Washington	ONE
$2	1928-1963A	Jefferson	Monticello
$5	1928-1963	Lincoln	Lincoln Memorial
$100	1966-1966A	Franklin	Indep. Hall

Small Size	F	XF
$1 1928	125.00	225.00
$2 1928A	20.00	75.00
$2 1928B	75.00	300.00
$2 1928C	20.00	65.00
$2 1928D	20.00	45.00
$2 1928E	30.00	50.00
$2 1928F	15.00	25.00
$2 1928G	10.00	25.00
$2 1953	10.00	15.00
$2 1953A	8.00	12.00
$2 1953B	7.00	10.00
$2 1953C	7.00	10.00
$2 1963	7.00	15.00
$2 1963A	7.00	9.00
$5 1928	15.00	35.00
$5 1928A	20.00	50.00
$5 1928B	15.00	30.00
$5 1928C	13.00	30.00
$5 1928D	40.00	75.00

Small Size	F	XF
$5 1928E	15.00	25.00
$5 1928F	10.00	50.00
$5 1953	10.00	15.00
$5 1953A	10.00	18.00
$5 1953B	10.00	15.00
$5 1953C	10.00	25.00
$5 1963	8.00	15.00
$100 1966	125.00	240.00
$100 1966A	150.00	200.00

GOLD CERTIFICATES

As the title on these notes implies, gold certificates were backed by reserves of gold coin and payable to the bearer in gold coin. The first gold certificates were issued from 1865 to 1875 but were used only for transactions between banks. Notes of this period not listed here are not known to have survived. The issue of 1882 was the first for general circulation. Only $5,000 and $10,000 notes were issued in 1888-1889 and did not circulate widely.

Regular issues were again placed in circulation from 1905 to 1907. Gold certificates of Series 1913-1928 are the most common. Gold certificates were reduced in size beginning with Series 1928. The small-size notes have a gold Treasury seal.

The final gold certificates, of 1934, were again issued just for bank transactions. The government recalled these notes from general circulation in 1933 when it withdrew gold coinage. Today, they are legal to own but are scarce because of the recall.

Large Size, First Issue, 1863	F	XF
$20 eagle on shield	—	500,000.00
$100 eagle on shield, rare	—	—

Large Size, Second Issue, 1870-71

No notes known to have survived.

Large Size, Third Issue, 1875

	F	XF
$100 Thomas H. Benton, rare	—	—

Large Size, 4th Issue, Series of 1882

	F	XF
$20 James Garfield, brown seal	2,500.00	7,500.00
$20 same, red seal	575.00	2,800.00
$50 Silas Wright	1,550.00	5,000.00
$100 Thomas Benton, brown seal, rare	—	—
$100 same, large red seal, rare	—	—
$100 same, small red seal	1,150.00	3,500.00
$500 Abraham Lincoln	10,500.00	25,000.00
$1,000 Alexander Hamilton, brown seal, 1 known	—	—
$1,000 same, large red seal, 1 known	—	—
$1,000 same, small red seal	—	230,000.00
$5,000 James Madison, rare	—	—
$10,000 Andrew Jackson, rare	—	—

Large Size, 5th Issue, Series of 1888

	F	XF
$10,000 Andrew Jackson, rare	—	—

Large Size, 6th Issue, Series of 1900

	F	XF
$10,000 Andrew Jackson	1,750.00	3,750.00

Large Size, 7th Issue, Series 1905-07

	F	XF
$10 1907 Michael Hillegas	175.00	500.00
$20 1905 George Washington	1,000.00	15,000.00
$20 1906 George Washington	200.00	650.00

Large Size, 8th Issue, Series of 1907

	F	XF
$1,000 Alexander Hamilton	15,000.00	37,500.00

Large Size, 9th Issue, Series of 1913

	F	XF
$10,000 Andrew Jackson, rare	—	—

Large Size, 10th Issue, Series of 1922

	F	XF
$10 Michael Hillegas	140.00	800.00
$20 George Washington	200.00	525.00
$50 Ulysses S. Grant	425.00	1,625.00
$100 Thomas Benton	700.00	3,000.00
$500 Abraham Lincoln	—	50,000.00
$1,000 Alexander Hamilton	—	80,500.00

Small Size, Series of 1928	F	XF
$10 Alexander Hamilton	145.00	200.00
$20 Andrew Jackson	155.00	250.00
$50 Ulysses S. Grant	600.00	900.00
$100 Benjamin Franklin	650.00	1,750.00
$500 William McKinley	9,000.00	15,000.00
$1,000 Grover Cleveland	8,000.00	15,000.00
$5,000 James Madison, 1 known	—	—

SILVER CERTIFICATES

On February 28, 1878, the same day Congress authorized the striking of millions of silver dollars, it also passed legislation authorizing silver certificates. The notes represented actual silver dollars held by the U.S. Treasury. The legislation passed in response to lobbying by silver-mining interests.

Some of the most famous and beautiful bank notes issued by the United States are silver certificates. These include the "educational" $1, $2, and $5 notes of 1896; the "One Papa" $5; and the "porthole" $5. "One Papa" is a misnomer. The note actually depicts Chief Running Antelope of the Uncpapa Sioux, but because the name was unfamiliar to early collectors, it was mispronounced "Chief One Papa."

Like other U.S. paper money, silver certificates were reduced in size with Series 1928, in 1929.

During World War II, there was fear that supplies of U.S. currency would fall into enemy hands if certain territories were lost. In response, notes distributed in these territories were given distinguishing features that permitted their identification and repudiation if captured. Silver certificates issued to troops in North Africa were printed with a yellow Treasury seal instead of a blue one. Notes distributed in Hawaii featured the word "Hawaii" overprinted in large letters on the back.

The motto "In God We Trust" was added to the $1 note for Series 1935G and 1935H, and all 1957 series. Silver certificates continued until Series 1957B, in 1963. Small-size silver certificates are occasionally found in circulation today and are easily recognized by their blue Treasury seal. When worn, these notes are generally not collectible but do have some novelty value. They have not been redeemable for silver dollars since 1968.

This series includes popular "star notes," which have part of the serial number replaced by a star. They were printed to replace notes accidentally destroyed in the manufacturing process. Star notes were introduced in 1899. They often, but not always, are worth somewhat more than regularly numbered pieces.

Large Size	F	XF
$1 1886 Martha Washington, small red seal	250.00	500.00
$1 1886 same, large red seal	300.00	550.00
$1 1886 same, brown seal	250.00	700.00
$1 1891 Martha Washington	275.00	800.00
$1 1896 History instructing youth	350.00	800.00
$1 1899 eagle	150.00	225.00
$1 1923 George Washington	35.00	60.00
$2 1886 Gen. Winfield Scott Hancock, small red seal	600.00	1,500.00
$2 1886 same, large red seal	500.00	1,500.00
$2 1886 same, brown seal	500.00	2,100.00
$2 1891 William Windom	475.00	1,800.00

Large Size	F	XF
$2 1896 Science presenting steam and electricity to Commerce and Industry	625.00	2,550.00
$2 1899 George Washington, Mechanics and Agriculture	200.00	500.00
$5 1886 Ulysses S. Grant, small red seal	1,250.00	5,000.00
$5 1886 same, large red seal	1,000.00	4,500.00
$5 1886 same, brown seal	1,300.00	4,250.00
$5 1891 Ulysses S. Grant	500.00	1,500.00
$5 1896 winged Electricity lighting the world 650	4,500.00	50,000.00
$5 1899 Chief Running Antelope	450.00	1,200.00
$5 1923 Abraham Lincoln	650.00	2,300.00
$10 1878 Robert Morris	—	40,000.00
$10 1880 same, brown seal	1,700.00	8,500.00
$10 1880 same, red seal	3,500.00	20,000.00
$10 1886 Thomas Hendricks, small red seal	1,250.00	5,000.00
$10 1886 same, large red seal	1,250.00	4,000.00
$10 1886 same, brown seal	1,000.00	5,000.00
$10 1891 Thomas Hendricks	600.00	2,000.00
$20 1878 Capt. Stephen Decatur	5,000.00	25,000.00
$20 1880 same	7,500.00	20,000.00
$20 1880 same, brown seal	3,000.00	11,000.00
$20 1880 same, red seal	6,000.00	22,000.00
$20 1886 Daniel Manning, small red seal	—	35,000.00
$20 1886 same, large red seal	5,000.00	50,000.00
$20 1886 same, brown seal	3,000.00	16,000.00

Large Size	F	XF
$20 1891 same, red seal	1,000.00	3,750.00
$20 1891 same, blue seal	700.00	3,450.00
$50 1878 Edward Everett	—	CU 37,000.00
$50 1880 same, brown seal	10,000.00	35,000.00
$50 1880 same, red seal	27,500.00	52,500.00
$50 1891 same, red seal	2,500.00	7,000.00
$50 1891 same, blue seal	1,500.00	6,600.00
$100 1878 James Monroe, rare	—	—
$100 1880 same, brown seal	16,000.00	45,000.00
$100 1800 same, red seal	—	125,000.00
$100 1891 same	8,000.00	43,125.00
$500 1878 Charles Sumner, rare	—	
$500 1880 same	—	420,000.00
$1,000 1878, William Marcy, none known		
$1,000 1880 William Marcy	—	580,000.00
$1,000 1891 Liberty, Marcy, rare	—	—

SMALL-SIZE SILVER CERTIFICATES, BLUE SEAL

Denom.	Series	Front	Back
$1	1928-1928E	Washington	ONE
$1	1934-1957B	Washington	Great Seal
$5	1934-1953C	Lincoln	Lincoln Memorial
$10	1933-1953B	Hamilton	Treasury

Small Size, Blue Seal	F	XF
$1 1928	25.00	50.00
$1 1928A	25.00	45.00
$1 1928B	25.00	45.00
$1 1928C	125.00	450.00
$1 1928D	60.00	200.00
$1 1928E	400.00	1,100.00
$1 1934	25.00	40.00
$1 1935	10.00	15.00
$1 1935A	3.00	6.00
$1 1935A "Hawaii"	45.00	70.00
$1 1935A yellow seal	45.00	95.00
$1 1935A red R	75.00	130.00
$1 1935A red S	75.00	150.00
$1 1935B	3.00	5.00
$1 1935C	2.00	4.00
$1 1935D	3.00	6.00
$1 1935E	3.00	4.00
$1 1935F	3.00	4.00
$1 1935G	3.00	5.00
$1 1935G "In God We Trust"	3.00	10.00
$1 1935H	3.00	5.00
$1 1957	3.00	4.00
$1 1957A	3.00	4.00
$1 1957B	3.00	4.00
$5 1934	15.00	40.00
$5 1934 "Hawaii"	75.00	200.00
$5 1934A	15.00	30.00
$5 1934A yellow seal	70.00	100.00
$5 1934B	10.00	25.00
$5 1934C	10.00	30.00
$5 1934D	10.00	20.00
$5 1953	10.00	25.00
$5 1953A	8.00	15.00
$5 1953B	8.00	15.00
$10 1933	3,500.00	7,000.00
$10 1934	30.00	60.00
$10 1934A	35.00	125.00
$10 1934 yellow seal	3,200.00	9,000.00
$10 1934A yellow seal	320.00	400.00
$10 1934B	160.00	350.00
$10 1934C	20.00	50.00

Small Size, Blue Seal	F	XF
$10 1934D	30.00	40.00
$10 1953	30.00	75.00
$10 1953A	40.00	125.00
$10 1953B	25.00	75.00

FEDERAL RESERVE NOTES

The Federal Reserve System was created in 1913. It consists of 12 Federal Reserve banks governed in part by the U.S. government through the Federal Reserve Board, whose members are appointed by the president and confirmed by the Senate. Each of the Federal Reserve banks is composed of various member banks.

The paper money used today in the United States is issued by the Federal Reserve banks. Originally, Federal Reserve notes could be redeemed for gold. That changed in 1934.

Like all other U.S. paper money, Federal Reserve notes were reduced in size with Series 1928, in 1929.

Since 1993, new anticounterfeiting innovations have been added to the notes. Micro printing was incorporated in the design and around the frame of the portrait. Also, a transparent strip bearing the value and "USA" was embedded in the paper. It can be seen only when the note is held up to a light and cannot be photocopied.

These improvements were precursors to the first major overhaul of U.S. paper money since the 1920s. Beginning with the $100 bill in 1996, more changes were made, including larger portraits to show more detail and more white space on the reverse so watermarks could be added to the paper.

A watermark is an image pressed against the paper while the newly printed note is drying. Like the transparent printed strip, it can be seen only when the note is held up to a light.

Among the most ingenious high-tech safeguards on the new notes is color-shifting ink, which alters its color depending on the angle of the light hitting it. The green Treasury seal has been retained, but the old letter seal indicating the Federal Reserve bank of distribution was replaced by the Federal Reserve System seal. These innovations were added to the $20 and $50 notes with Series 1996 and the $5 and $10 notes with Series 1999. The $1 note was not scheduled to change.

Starting in 2003, additional steps were taken to prevent counterfeiting. The $5, $10, $20, and $50 notes received multicolored background designs. The changes are also slated for the $100 note.

Federal Reserve notes are produced at the Bureau of Engraving and Printing's main facility in Washington, D.C., and at its Western Currency Facility in Fort Worth,

Texas. Notes produced at Fort Worth have a small "FW" mark in the lower right corner of the face.

Most Federal Reserve notes produced since the 1930s are collected only in high grade. Dealers may be unwilling to buy even scarce pieces if they are not crisp uncirculated. Star notes, which have a star instead of one of the numerals in their serial numbers, are popularly collected in this series but, again, must be crisp to be desirable. Recent issues command no premium; they are sold at face value plus a handling fee to cover the dealer's costs.

For Series of 1988A, 1993, and 1995 $1 Federal Reserve notes, the BEP experimented with web presses for printing the notes. On web presses, the paper is fed into the presses on rolls. Traditionally, paper money has been printed on sheet-fed presses. The web-press $1 Federal Reserve notes can be distinguished from the regular notes in two ways: (1) On the front of regularly printed notes, there is a small letter and number to the lower right of the Treasury seal indicating the plate number. On web-printed notes, there will be only a number with no letter preceding it. (2) On the back of regularly printed notes, the plate number appears to the lower right of the "E" in "One." On web-printed notes, the number appears above the "E" in "One."

Large Size, Red Seal, Series of 1914	F	XF
$5 Abraham Lincoln	300.00	600.00
$10 Andrew Jackson	400.00	1,250.00
$20 Grover Cleveland	400.00	2,000.00
$50 Ulysses S. Grant	2,750.00	4,500.00
$100 Benjamin Franklin	1,750.00	3,750.00

Large Size, Blue Seal, Series of 1914	F	XF
$5 Abraham Lincoln	60.00	150.00
$10 Andrew Jackson	85.00	250.00
$20 Grover Cleveland	215.00	400.00
$50 Ulysses S. Grant	200.00	700.00
$100 Benjamin Franklin	400.00	1,250.00

Large Size, Blue Seal, Series of 1918	F	XF
$500 John Marshall	7,000.00	30,000.00
$1,000 Alexander Hamilton	10,000.00	20,000.00
$5,000 James Madison, rare	—	—
$10,000 Salmon P. Chase, rare	—	—

SMALL-SIZE NOTES, GREEN SEAL

Denom.	Issue	Front	Back
$1	1963	Washington	Great Seal
$2	1976	Jefferson	Signing Declaration
$5	1928	Lincoln	Lincoln Memorial
$10	1928	Hamilton	Treasury Building
$20	1928	Jackson	White House
$50	1928	Grant	Capitol
$100	1928	Franklin	Independence Hall
$500	1928-1934A	McKinley	500
$1,000	1928-1934A	Cleveland	inscription
$5,000	1928-1934B	Madison	5,000
$10,000	1928-1934B	Chase	10,000

	XF	CU
$1 1963	3.00	6.00
$1 1963A	3.00	5.00
$1 1963B	3.00	9.00
$1 1969	2.00	7.00
$1 1969A	2.00	5.00
$1 1969B	2.00	5.00
$1 1969C	3.00	7.00
$1 1969D	2.00	7.00

	XF	CU
$1 1974	2.00	5.00
$1 1977	2.00	6.00
$1 1977A	2.00	6.00
$1 1981	2.00	7.00
$1 1981A	2.00	6.00
$1 1985	—	6.00
$1 1988	2.00	9.00
$1 1988A	2.00	6.00
$1 1988A web press	7.75	40.00
$1 1993	2.00	6.00
$1 1993 web press	6.00	15.00
$1 1995	—	4.00
$1 1995 FW	—	4.00
$1 1995 web press	8.00	17.00
$1 1999	—	3.00
$1 1999 FW	—	3.00
$1 2001	—	3.00
$1 2001 FW	—	3.00
$1 2003	—	3.00
$1 2003 FW	—	3.00
$1 2003A	—	3.00
$1 2003A FW	—	3.00
$1 2006	—	3.00
$1 2006 FW	—	3.00
$1 2009	—	3.00
$1 2009 FW	—	3.00
$2 1976	3.00	10.00
$2 1995	4.00	9.00
$2 2003 FW	—	9.00
$2 2003A FW	—	8.00

	F	XF
$5 1928	20.00	100.00
$5 1928A	15.00	75.00
$5 1928B	12.00	25.00
$5 1928C	500.00	1,500.00
$5 1928D	750.00	2,500.00

	F	XF
$5 1934	10.00	20.00
$5 1934 "Hawaii"	75.00	200.00
$5 1934A	10.00	20.00
$5 1934B	10.00	20.00
$5 1934C	10.00	20.00
$5 1934D	10.00	20.00
$5 1950	8.00	12.00
$5 1950A	10.00	18.00
$5 1950B	10.00	20.00
$5 1950C	8.00	10.00
$5 1950D	8.00	10.00
$5 1950E	15.00	25.00
$5 1963	8.00	10.00
$5 1963A	8.00	10.00
$5 1969	6.00	7.00
$5 1969A	6.00	8.00
$5 1969B	10.00	30.00

	XF	CU
$5 1969C	7.00	20.00
$5 1974	7.00	15.00
$5 1977	7.00	15.00
$5 1977A	10.00	35.00
$5 1981	8.00	25.00
$5 1981A	15.00	30.00
$5 1985	7.00	15.00
$5 1988	7.00	15.00
$5 1988A	7.00	15.00
$5 1988A FW	7.00	15.00
$5 1993	7.00	15.00
$5 1993	7.00	15.00
$5 1995	6.00	10.00
$5 1995 FW	—	10.00
$5 1999	6.00	10.00
$5 1999 FW	6.00	10.00
$5 2001	7.00	15.00
$5 2003	7.00	15.00
$5 2003 FW	7.00	15.00
$5 2003A FW	7.00	15.00
$5 2006 FW	7.00	15.00
$5 2006 FW colorized	7.00	15.00

	F	XF
$10 1928	35.00	125.00
$10 1928A	35.00	60.00
$10 1928B	18.00	30.00
$10 1928C	65.00	225.00
$10 1934	15.00	40.00
$10 1934A	11.00	12.00
$10 1934A "Hawaii"	100.00	275.00
$10 1934B	13.00	25.00
$10 1934C	11.00	15.00
$10 1934D	11.00	20.00

	XF	CU
$10 1950	20.00	75.00
$10 1950A	30.00	70.00
$10 1950B	20.00	35.00
$10 1950C	30.00	50.00
$10 1950D	20.00	50.00
$10 1950E	55.00	125.00
$10 1963	15.00	50.00
$10 1963A	20.00	50.00
$10 1969	15.00	40.00
$10 1969A	15.00	45.00
$10 1969B	50.00	150.00
$10 1969C	20.00	40.00
$10 1974	15.00	35.00
$10 1977	15.00	35.00
$10 1977A	15.00	35.00
$10 1981	20.00	40.00
$10 1981A	20.00	40.00
$10 1985	20.00	35.00
$10 1988A	20.00	35.00
$10 1990	—	20.00
$10 1993	—	20.00
$10 1995	—	20.00
$10 1999	—	20.00
$10 1999 FW	—	20.00
$10 2001	—	20.00
$10 2001 FW	—	20.00

	XF	CU
$10 2003	—	15.00
$10 2003 FW	—	15.00
$10 2004A FW	—	15.00
$10 2006 FW	—	15.00
$10 2009 FW	—	15.00

	F	XF
$20 1928	50.00	125.00
$20 1928A	60.00	150.00
$20 1928B	30.00	50.00
$20 1928C	225.00	700.00
$20 1934	225.00	700.00
$20 1934 "Hawaii"	700.00	2,000
$20 1934A	25.00	35.00
$20 1934B	25.00	35.00
$20 1934C	25.00	40.00

	XF	CU
$20 1934D	30.00	95.00
$20 1950	35.00	70.00
$20 1950A	30.00	70.00
$20 1950B	30.00	60.00
$20 1950C	35.00	50.00
$20 1950D	35.00	75.00
$20 1950E	25.00	70.00
$20 1963	35.00	75.00
$20 1963A	30.00	60.00
$20 1969	30.00	60.00
$20 1969A	40.00	80.00
$20 1969B	100.00	200.00
$20 1969C	30.00	60.00
$20 1974	30.00	55.00
$20 1977	30.00	60.00
$20 1981	35.00	75.00
$20 1981A	30.00	60.00
$20 1985	25.00	50.00
$20 1988A	30.00	60.00
$20 1990	25.00	45.00
$20 1993	—	40.00
$20 1993 FW	—	40.00
$20 1995	—	45.00
$20 1995 FW	—	45.00
$20 1996	—	30.00

	XF	CU
$20 1996 FW	—	30.00
$20 1999	—	30.00
$20 1999 FW	—	30.00
$20 2001	—	30.00
$20 2001 FW	—	30.00
$20 2004	—	30.00
$20 2004 FW	—	30.00
$20 2004A	—	30.00
$20 2004A FW	—	30.00
$20 2006	—	30.00
$20 2006 FW	—	30.00
$20 2009	—	30.00
$20 2009 FW	—	30.00

	F	XF
$50 1928	100.00	250.00
$50 1928A	70.00	100.00
$50 1934	—	60.00
$50 1934A	75.00	125.00
$50 1934B	70.00	125.00
$50 1934C	75.00	110.00
$50 1934D	75.00	110.00
$50 1950	80.00	100.00
$50 1950A	75.00	100.00
$50 1950B	60.00	80.00
$50 1950C	50.00	70.00
$50 1950D	55.00	100.00
$50 1950E	100.00	150.00

	XF	CU
$50 1963A	75.00	80.00
$50 1969	60.00	100.00
$50 1969A	75.00	100.00
$50 1969B	700.00	1,000
$50 1969C	65.00	75.00
$50 1974	70.00	115.00
$50 1977	55.00	75.00
$50 1981	70.00	115.00
$50 1981A	75.00	100.00
$50 1985	60.00	75.00
$50 1988	60.00	150.00
$50 1990	—	75.00
$50 1993	—	70.00

	XF	CU
$50 1996	—	60.00
$50 2001	—	70.00
$50 2004 FW	—	70.00
$50 2004A FW	—	70.00
$50 2006 FW	—	75.00
$50 2009 FW	—	75.00

	XF	CU
$100 1928	250.00	750.00
$100 1928A	200.00	350.00
$100 1934	130.00	200.00
$100 1934A	180.00	400.00
$100 1934B	300.00	450.00
$100 1934C	200.00	400.00
$100 1934D	350.00	500.00
$100 1950	200.00	400.00
$100 1950A	—	240.00
$100 1950B	185.00	200.00
$100 1950C	—	200.00
$100 1950D	—	200.00
$100 1950E	200.00	300.00
$100 1963A	—	150.00
$100 1969	—	140.00
$100 1969A	—	180.00
$100 1969C	—	150.00
$100 1974	—	135.00
$100 1977	—	130.00
$100 1981	—	140.00
$100 1981A	125.00	160.00
$100 1985	—	150.00
$100 1988	—	175.00
$100 1990	—	150.00
$100 1993	—	160.00
$100 1996	—	120.00
$100 1999	—	125.00
$100 2001	—	125.00
$100 2003	—	135.00

	XF	CU
$100 2003A	—	125.00
$100 2006	—	125.00
$100 2006 FW	—	125.00
$100 2006A	—	125.00
$100 2009	—	—
$100 2009 FW	—	—

	F	XF
$500 1928	850.00	1,300.00
$500 1934	750.00	1,250.00
$500 1934A	750.00	1,150.00
$500 1934B, specimens only	—	—
$500 1934C, specimens only	—	—
$1,000 1928	1,600.00	2,000.00
$1,000 1934	1,500.00	2,000.00
$1,000 1934A	1,500.00	2,000.00
$1,000 1934C, specimens only	—	—
$5,000 1928	20,000.00	105,000.00
$5,000 1934	20,000.00	70,000.00
$5,000 1934A, rare	—	—
$5,000 1934B, rare	—	—
$10,000 1928	—	170,000.00
$10,000 1934	46,000.00	70,000.00
$10,000 1934A, specimens only	—	—
$10,000 1934B, none known	—	—